BTEC
FIRST

endorsed for
BTEC

D0315808

CHILDREN'S PLAY, LEARNING AND DEVELOPMENT

ALWAYS LEARNING

Library
Coleg Gŵyr Abertawe
Llyrfgell

PEARSON

Published by Pearson Education Limited, Edinburgh Gate, Harlow, Essex, CM20 2JE.

www.pearsonschoolsandfecolleges.co.uk

Text © Penny Tassoni 2013
Typeset by Phoenix Photosetting, Chatham, Kent, UK
Original illustrations © Pearson Education Limited 2013
Illustrated by Katie Mac/NB Illustration Ltd and Phoenix Photosetting
Cover design by Pearson Education Limited and Andrew Magee Design
Front cover photo: Masterfile UK Ltd
Indexing by Catherine Harkness

The right of Penny Tassoni to be identified as author of this work has been asserted by her in accordance with the Copyright, Designs and Patents Act 1988.

18 17
10 9 8 7 6 5

British Library Cataloguing in Publication Data
A catalogue record for this book is available from the British Library

ISBN 978 1 447944 61 4

Copyright notice
All rights reserved. No part of this publication may be reproduced in any form or by any means (including photocopying or storing it in any medium by electronic means and whether or not transiently or incidentally to some other use of this publication) without the written permission of the copyright owner, except in accordance with the provisions of the Copyright, Designs and Patents Act 1988 or under the terms of a licence issued by the Copyright Licensing Agency, Saffron House, 6–10 Kirby Street, London EC1N 8TS (www.cla.co.uk). Applications for the copyright owner's written permission should be addressed to the publisher.

Printed and bound in Italy by L.E.G.O S.p.A

Websites
There are links to relevant websites in this book. In order to ensure that the links are up to date, that the links work, and that the sites aren't inadvertently links to sites that could be considered offensive, we have made the links available on our website at www.pearsonhotlinks.co.uk. Search for the title 'BTEC First Children's Play, Learning and Development Student Book' or ISBN 978 1 447944 61 4.

Copies of official specifications for all Pearson qualifications may be found on the website: www.edexcel.com

A note from the publisher
In order to ensure that this resource offers high-quality support for the associated BTEC Pearson qualification, it has been through a review process by the awarding organisation to confirm that it fully covers the teaching and learning content of the specification or part of a specification at which it is aimed, and demonstrates an appropriate balance between the development of subject skills, knowledge and understanding, in addition to preparation for assessment.

While the publishers have made every attempt to ensure that advice on the qualification and its assessment is accurate, the official specification and associated assessment guidance materials are the only authoritative source of information and should always be referred to for definitive guidance.

BTEC examiners have not contributed to any sections in this resource relevant to examination papers for which they have responsibility.

No material from an endorsed book will be used verbatim in any assessment set by BTEC.

Endorsement of a book does not mean that the book is required to achieve this BTEC qualification, nor does it mean that it is the only suitable material available to support the qualification, and any resource lists produced by the awarding organisation shall include this and other appropriate resources.

ACC. No: GCS 041349

GOWER COLLEGE SWANSEA
LEARNING RESOURCE CENTRE

CLASS No: 362.7 TAS

Acknowledgements

The publisher would like to thank the following for their kind permission to reproduce their photographs:

(Key: b-bottom; c-centre; l-left; r-right; t-top)

Alamy Images: Bubbles Photolibrary 48-U2, 79-U3, Bubbles Photolibrary 48-U2, 79-U3, Gaetano Images 102-U4, Gary Roebuck 150-U5, Picture Partners 113-U4; **Bananastock:** 157-U5; **Brand X Pictures:** www.agefotostock.com. SuperStock. 165-U6; **British Standards Institution:** 146-U5cr; **DK Images:** Andy Crawford 139-U5, Dave King -U1, Vanessa Davies 61-U2, 122-U4, 136-U5, 212-U8, Vanessa Davis 46-U2, Victoria Blackie 145-U5; **Getty Images:** Fotosearch Value 188-U7, Greg Samborski 85-U3, Jacqueline Veissid 20-U1, Jay P. Morgan 140-U5, Mel Yates 52-U2, Svenne Nordlov 57-U2, Tim Laman 194-U7; **Imagestate Media:** BananaStock 200-U7, 224-U8; **Pearson Education Ltd:** Sophie Bluy 1-U1, Debbie Rowe 64-U2, Handan Erek 158-U6, 182-U7, Gareth Boden 37-U1, 70-U3, 98-U4, 208-U8, Jules Selmes -U3, -U4, -U5, -U8, -U2, 3-U1, 7-U1, 11-U1, 19-U1, 25-U1, 29-U1, 31-U1t, 33-U1, 36-U1, 42-U2, 43-U2, 45-U2, 51-U2, 55-U2, 58-U2, 59-U2, 66-U2, 67-U2, 71-U3, 74-U3, 75-U3, 76-U3, 79-U3t, 83-U3, 86-U3, 89-U3, 90-U3, 92-U3, 94-U3, 99-U4, 104-U4, 107-U4, 111-U4, 118-U4, 133-U5, 135-U5, 146-U5t, 146-U5b, 159-U6, 164-U6, 166-U6, 172-U6, 175-U6, 183-U7, 192-U7, 203-U7, 205-U7, 209-U8, 211-U8, 219-U8, 225-U8, Lord and Leverett 167-U6, MindStudio 207-U7, Roddy Paine 17-U1, Studio 8 82-U3, 109-U4, 126-U4, 132-U5, 163-U6, 169-U6, 214-U8, Tsz-shan Kwok 147-U5, Tudor Photography -U6, 161-U6; **Shutterstock.com:** Diego Cervo 35-U1, iofoto 229-U8, Maxriesgo 189-U7b, Snow white images 97-U3; **Studio 8:** 24-U1, 31-U1; **The British Toy & Hobby Association:** 146-U5cl; **Veer/Corbis:** Avava 181-U6, Izarizhar -U7, 185-U7, Naumoid 49-U2, PT Images 127-U4, Shell114 69-U2, Smit 189-U7, viki2win 151-U5

Cover images: *Front:* Masterfile UK Ltd

All other images © Pearson Education

The author and publisher would like to thank the following individuals and organisations for permission to reproduce their materials:

p. 153 Clean your hands campaign poster. Reproduced, with permission, from the NHS/National Patient Safety Agency.

Every effort has been made to trace the copyright holders and we apologise in advance for any unintentional omissions. We would be pleased to insert the appropriate acknowledgement in any subsequent edition of this publication.

The BTEC First Award in Children's Play, Learning and Development will give you the fundamental knowledge and understanding of child development and of promoting development through play. Students taking the Certificate will also have the opportunity to develop a broader understanding of the early years sector, including health and safety, supporting children's language and literacy development, nutrition for children, as well as roles, responsibilities and career pathways in the sector. A BTEC First CPLD qualification can also help you to progress to the next level of study.

About the author

Best-selling author Penny Tassoni trained as an early years and primary teacher. Now working as an education consultant and trainer, she specialises in the whole spectrum of learning and play. Penny has written over 30 books about early years and she frequently writes articles for national early years magazines. She is also a respected speaker and works nationally and internationally in this role. In addition, Penny is President for the Professional Association for Childcare and Early Years (PACEY). She has in-depth knowledge of the BTEC Firsts in Children's Play, Learning and Development and uses her accessible and friendly style of writing to bring the information to life for learners on this course.

This book contains many features that will help you use your skills and knowledge in work-related situations, and assist you in getting the most from your course.

Introduction

These introductions give you a snapshot of what to expect from each unit – and what you should be aiming for by the time you finish it.

How this unit is assessed.

Learning aims describe what you will be doing in the unit.

A learner shares their experience in relation to the unit.

Features of this book

There are lots of features in this book to help you learn about the topics in each unit, and to have fun while learning! These pages show some of the features that you will come across when using the book.

Learning aim and topic references show which parts of the BTEC you are covering on these pages.

Discussion point, with a short activity or discussion about the topic.

Key terms appear in blue bold text and are defined either within the text or in a key term box on the page. Also see the glossary for definitions of important words and phrases.

Activity 4.1

Harry is 4 years old. He attends a nursery where he is very happy. Today his mother has let the nursery know that he did not sleep well last night. He also did not want to eat his breakfast. He is now hungry. Harry has just thrown a book across the room. This is not how he normally behaves.

1 What are the factors that are affecting Harry's behaviour?

2 Explain how Harry's needs link to Maslow's theory.

Activities will help you learn about the topic. These will be done in pairs or groups, or sometimes on your own.

Assessment practice 1.2

You will need to explain how one area of development can be affected by the delay of another.

For each of the five areas of development, give an example of how it might be affected by an aspect of another area of development. An example of how physical development can be affected by emotional development has been done for you.

1 Physical development *can be affected by emotional development – if children are not confident, they might not try out new skills.*

2 Cognitive development

3 Language development

4 Social development

5 Emotional development

A chance to practise answering the types of test questions that you may come across in your exam. (For Units 1 and 4.)

Assessment activity 3.2

2B.P3 | 2B.M2 | 2B.D2

You have been asked to find out about how inclusive practice can be implemented in early years settings. You are to write a report about this. Choose an early years setting to visit or ask someone about how they implement inclusive practice in their setting.

Your report should include:

- ways in which it is possible for early years settings to implement inclusive practice
- how the early years setting that you have learned about implements inclusive practice, and how successful it is in doing this.

Tip

- Try to give examples of how inclusive practice is implemented. These examples should be from the early years setting that you have researched. You should also discuss how successfully the setting is implementing inclusive practice. To do this, think about what they are doing well, as well as how they could improve, making sure you consider all the relevant factors and which are the most important.

Activities that relate to the unit's assessment criteria. These activities will help you prepare for your assignments and contain tips to help you achieve your potential. (For all units **except** Units 1 and 4.)

Just checking

1 What is meant by the term 'role model'?

2 Which theory suggests that meeting children's basic physical needs is important so they can show wanted behaviour?

3 What is the link between sleep and children's behaviour?

4 How might communication and language delay affect children's behaviour?

5 Why might feeling unwell affect children's behaviour?

Use these to check your knowledge and understanding of the topic you have just covered.

Someone who works in the early years sector explains how this unit of the BTEC First applies to the day-to-day work they do as part of their job.

WorkSpace

▷ Lin Chapman

Pre-school supervisor

I have been working at this pre-school for ten years now. I am responsible for the smooth running of the setting. We have many volunteers and work experience students come here on placement. I try to help them understand the principles behind how we work. It is known as being a happy place. We pride ourselves on being an inclusive setting. This means looking for ways to make sure that everyone, feels that they are welcome, especially families and children, and also that their thoughts, ideas and needs are important to us. As part of this, we spend a lot of time talking and listening to families about their needs and ideas, but also to the children themselves. We want children to feel that they are special and that their ideas count too. We therefore look for ways of letting children make choices about what they want to do and play with. We also encourage children to do as much as they can for themselves so that they can gain in confidence. Alongside this, every child has a key person – someone special who spends time with them and really gets to know them.

Think about it

1 What have you learnt about in this unit that links to this pre-school's way of working?

2 Explain how this pre-school is empowering children.

3 Why do you think that this pre-school is known as being a happy place?

This section also gives you the chance to think more about the role that this person does, and whether you would want to follow in their footsteps once you've completed your studies.

BTEC Assessment Zone

You will be assessed in two different ways for your BTEC First in Children's Play, Learning and Development. For most units, your teacher/tutor will set assignments for you to complete. These may take the form of projects where you research, plan, prepare, and evaluate a piece of work or activity. The table in this BTEC Assessment Zone explains what you must do in order to achieve each of the assessment criteria. Each unit of this book contains a number of assessment activities to help you with these assessment criteria.

> The table in the BTEC Assessment Zone explains what you must do in order to achieve each of the assessment criteria, and signposts assessment activities in this book to help you to prepare for your assignments.

Assessment criteria			
Level 1	Level 2 Pass	Level 2 Merit	Level 2 Distinction
Learning aim A: Understand the importance of inclusive practice in early years			
1A.1 Outline three benefits to children of inclusive practice in early years settings.	**2A.P1** English Describe how children benefit from inclusive practice in early years settings. **See Assessment activity 3.1, page 80**	**2A.M1** English Explain the potential impact on children of inclusive and non-inclusive practice in early years settings, using appropriate examples. **See Assessment activity 3.1, page 80**	**2A.D1** English Compare how inclusive and non-inclusive practice affects children in early years settings, using case studies. **See Assessment activity 3.1, page 80**
1A.2 Outline three ways in which children may be affected by non-inclusive practice in early years settings.	**2A.P2** English Describe ways in which children may be affected by non-inclusive practice in early years settings. **See Assessment activity 3.1, page 80**		

> Activities in this book will show you the kinds of task you might be asked to do to meet these criteria when your teacher/tutor sets an assignment.

A Questions where you have to choose from several answers.

Tip: Read the question very carefully. Sometimes more than one answer is required.

Example:

Lack of exercise can affect children's behaviour, making them:

A tired	B frustrated	C lazy	D cheeky

Answer: B

Setting boundaries and expectations is important in order to promote positive behaviour. Of the following, which two **aren't** necessary?

A being aware of the age and stage of the children

B considering what the children are wearing

C explaining to the children the reasons behind the boundaries and expectations

D making a poster with rules for the children

Answers: B and D

> For Units 1 and 4 of your BTEC, you will be assessed by a paper-based exam. The BTEC Assessment Zone in Units 1 and 4 helps you to prepare for your exam by showing you some of the different types of questions you may need to answer.

Planning and getting organised

The first step in managing your time is to plan ahead and be well organised. Some people are naturally good at this. They think ahead, write down commitments in a diary or planner and store their notes and handouts neatly and carefully so they can find them quickly.

How good are your working habits?

Improving your planning and organisational skills

1 Use a diary to schedule working times into your weekdays and weekends.
2 Also use the diary to write down exactly what work you have to do. You could use this as a 'to do' list and tick off each task as you go.
3 Divide up long or complex tasks into manageable chunks and put each 'chunk' in your diary with a deadline of its own.
4 Always allow more time than you think you need for a task.

Take it further

If you become distracted by social networking sites or texts when you're working, set yourself a time limit of 10 minutes or so to indulge yourself. You could even use this as a reward for completing a certain amount of work.

Sources of information

You will need to use research to complete your BTEC First assignments, so it's important to know what sources of information are available to you. These are likely to include the following:

Remember!

Store relevant information when you find it – keep a folder on your computer specifically for research – so you don't have to worry about finding it again at a later date.

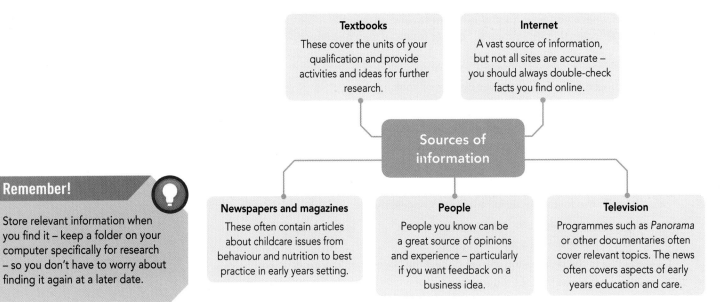

Textbooks
These cover the units of your qualification and provide activities and ideas for further research.

Internet
A vast source of information, but not all sites are accurate – you should always double-check facts you find online.

Sources of information

Newspapers and magazines
These often contain articles about childcare issues from behaviour and nutrition to best practice in early years setting.

People
People you know can be a great source of opinions and experience – particularly if you want feedback on a business idea.

Television
Programmes such as *Panorama* or other documentaries often cover relevant topics. The news often covers aspects of early years education and care.

▶ Organising and selecting information

Organising your information

Once you have used a range of sources of information for research, you will need to organise the information so it's easy to use.

- Make sure your written notes are neat and have a clear heading – it's often useful to date them, too.
- Always keep a note of where the information came from (the title of a book, the title and date of a newspaper or magazine and the web address of a website) and, if relevant, which pages.
- Work out the results of any questionnaires you've used.

Selecting your information

Once you have completed your research, re-read the assignment brief or instructions you were given to remind yourself of the exact wording of the question(s) and divide your information into three groups:

1 Information that is totally relevant.
2 Information that is not as good, but which could come in useful.
3 Information that doesn't match the questions or assignment brief very much, but that you kept because you couldn't find anything better!

Check that there are no obvious gaps in your information against the questions or assignment brief. If there are, make a note of them so that you know exactly what you still have to find.

▶ Presenting your work

Before handing in any assignments, make sure:

- you have addressed each part of the question and that your work is as complete as possible
- all spelling and grammar is correct
- you have referenced all sources of information you used for your research
- all work is your own – otherwise you could be committing **plagiarism**
- you have saved a copy of your work.

▶ Find out more

A range of activity sheets to help you develop the study skills you will use on your BTEC course is available. Go to www.pearsonhotlinks.co.uk, search for this title and click on the relevant section.

Alternatively, ask your teacher or tutor for more details.

Key term

Plagiarism – If you are including other people's views, comments or opinions, or copying a diagram or table from another publication, you must state the source by including the name of the author or publication, or the web address. Failure to do this (so you are really pretending other people's work is your own) is known as plagiarism. Check your school's policy on plagiarism and copying.

Introduction

Babies and young children are fascinating. Have you ever wondered why babies put things in their mouths? Or why 2 year olds often play alone, but 4 year olds love being with other children? This unit looks at child development and the patterns that can be seen in the way children grow and develop. It will help you to understand why children at particular ages and stages tend to do similar things. It is an essential unit if you wish to work with children and this is why it is the first unit in this book. All adults working with children need to know the patterns of child development because this helps them decide what types of toys, resources and activities will be suitable and safe to put out. More importantly, knowledge of the patterns of child development helps adults to know how they can support children at different ages. This knowledge is also used to recognise when children may need additional support because they are not showing typical patterns of development.

Assessment: This unit is assessed using a paper-based examination.

Learning aims

In this unit you will:

A understand growth and development in children

B understand the characteristics of children's development from birth up to eight years

C understand how adults in early years settings can support children's development.

> After I had finished this unit, I noticed more about what children do at different ages. I also felt more confident about working with children when I was on placement.
>
> Nikki, *16-year-old early years student*

Patterns of Child Development

1

▶ Growth and development

Discussion point

With a partner, talk about the factors that you feel might affect the growth of a child. Compare your ideas to those of others in the class.

Introduction

In this topic you will learn about the difference between growth and development and the factors affecting growth. You will also find out that development is made up of five separate areas.

Key terms

Growth – the division of cells.

Cell – a tiny part of the body.

Health visitors – health professionals who advise families with children.

Head circumference – the measurement of the head from above the eyebrows to around the back of the head.

Centile chart – a chart on which measurements are marked and compared with those of other children of the same age.

▶ Growth

'Haven't you grown?' This is what most adults say when they have not seen a child for a while. **Growth** is a major feature of childhood. Growth takes place because certain **cells** in the body keep dividing. This division of cells means that during childhood children increase in height and weight. Their bones become longer and so their skeleton changes. Growth also affects the development of muscles. Interestingly, during childhood the brain also grows.

How growth is measured

From birth onwards children are frequently measured by **health visitors**. Their height, weight and also **head circumference** are measured. The results are marked on a chart called a **centile chart**. The results form a graph which shows how much the child has grown and whether the growth is even. The centile chart also has bands on it showing where the child's growth is compared to children of the same age. Health professionals will often take time to look at children who are not growing as expected. This can sometimes be a sign of medical problems or it might be a sign that the child is not eating the right quantity or type of food.

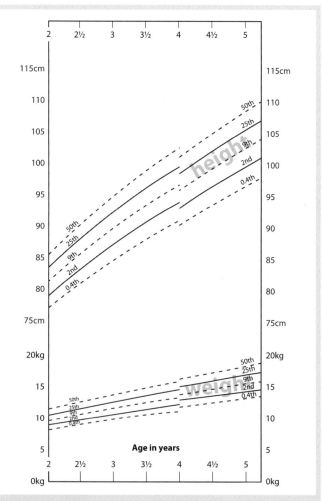

Figure 1.1 Centile chart showing girl's development from 2 to 5 years up to the 50th percentile.

Factors affecting growth

There are a wide range of factors that affect children's growth. Table 1.1 lists some of the main factors.

Table 1.1 Factors affecting children's growth.

Factor	How it affects children's growth
Heredity	Children's genetic make-up that they inherit from their biological parents will affect children's overall height. Some medical conditions affecting growth can also be inherited.
Hormones	**Hormones** are chemicals. They act as 'messengers' and tell cells when to divide. At certain stages in children's lives an increase in hormones will produce more rapid growth. A good example of this in young people is during puberty.
Nutrition	The body needs energy in order to grow. The body also needs a wide range of substances called **nutrients** in order for muscles, bones and organs to keep healthy, and also to grow. Children who are not eating a balanced diet may have uneven or insufficient growth.
Sleep	Sleep is important for growth. During sleep, hormones for growth are produced. Babies usually sleep between 12 and 14 hours a day, while young children will need at least 10 to 12 hours. Children who do not sleep well may have uneven growth.
Illness	Children who are frequently ill may not grow well. This is because they may not feel like eating or they may not be sleeping well. Some types of diseases can also make it hard for the digestion of nutrients to take place.
Emotional influences	There are many reasons why children may not be relaxed and happy. This includes separation of parents, the death of a close relative or not being settled in an early years setting. When children have long periods of unhappiness, they are less likely to sleep or eat well. They are also more likely to become ill.

Key terms

Hormones – chemicals that can trigger cell division, creating subsequent growth.

Nutrients – substances found in food that are essential for health and growth.

Development

The term 'development' is used to talk about the skills and knowledge that children gain. Over time, they gain skills and knowledge, such as being able to walk, draw a picture or count.

Holistic development

While all children develop, some will do so more quickly than others. Interestingly, children rarely acquire skills and knowledge evenly. A good example of this is a child aged 3 who might be able to name three colours but cannot yet kick a ball.

Take it further

Find out about how much sleep babies and young children need. You will need to download the publication *Information for Parents Booklet – Sleep*. Now go to www.pearsonhotlinks.co.uk, search for this title and click on this activity.

When early years practitioners and health visitors look at children's development, they tend to look at the whole picture of what a child can do. The term to describe this approach is **holistic development**.

Norms of development

When a baby starts to crawl, or when a child can say their name, these are special moments in their development. These are called **milestones**. For every age group, there is a list of milestones that most children will meet. These are the **developmental norms**. An example of a developmental norm is that by the age of 2, most children will say 50 or so words. Decisions about what to expect are based on looking at what most children do at a particular age. Looking at children's progress is usually done using the milestones for their age. Knowing about the milestones for each child can help you plan activities, but also help you spot any children who may need more support.

▶ Five key areas of development

As there are so many aspects involved in children's development, it is normally split into five broad areas as shown in Figure 1.2.

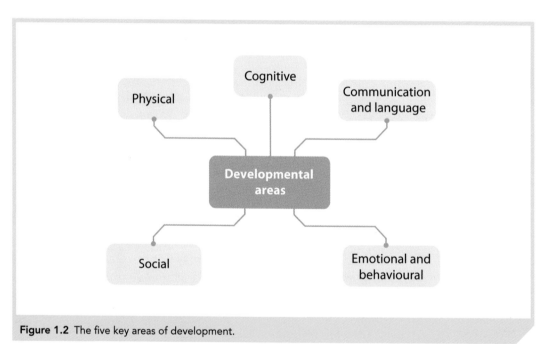

Figure 1.2 The five key areas of development.

Physical development

- This is about the way that children move and use their bodies. It is divided further into **gross motor movements** and **fine motor movements**.
- Gross motor movements involve use of the arms and legs. Kicking and throwing would be examples of gross motor movements. As part of gross motor movements, children also learn to be mobile. These movements are called **locomotive movements**. They involve balance and coordination.

Key terms

Holistic development – the development of a child, taking into account all aspects of what they can do, not just one single area of development.

Milestones – skills or pieces of knowledge that a child has acquired.

Developmental norms – the milestones that are associated with a particular age group.

Discussion point

In small groups, talk about how you developed as children.

- When did you learn to walk?
- Were you quick, slow or about average when learning to talk?
- How easily did you learn to read?
- How easily did you learn to throw and kick a ball?
- Why do you think that it can be hard to define an 'average' child?

Key terms

Gross motor movements – large movements of the arms and legs.

Fine motor movements – small movements usually associated with the hands.

Locomotive movements – skills involved in crawling, walking, running and being mobile.

- Fine motor movements are usually about the hands. There are many skills involved in fine motor movements. These include **hand–eye coordination**. This is where the hands and eyes work together, for example, in handwriting or sewing. Children's hands also have to develop strength and a range of movements called **fine manipulative movements**. These are quite complex or intricate. Being able to turn the lid of a bottle is an example of this; so too is the **tripod grasp**, sometimes known as the pencil grasp.

What gross motor skills is this child showing?

Cognitive development

This area of development is about the way that our brains take in information. This is called **perception**. It is also about the way that we remember and think about the information that we have taken in. Cognitive development is linked to imagination, problem solving and our understanding of concepts such as colour, number and shape.

Communication and language development

This is about being able to understand what others say, as well as being able to speak and make yourself understood. It is also about learning to read and write.

Emotional and behavioural development

This is about how children develop feelings and concern for others. It is also about how they learn to express their emotions, such as anger or excitement, appropriately. Emotional development also includes how we view ourselves (called **self-concept**) and whether we value ourselves (called **self-esteem**).

Social development

This is about our relationships with other people. It is about friendships with other children, but also the skills needed to maintain relationships, such as being thoughtful and cooperative and learning how to be part of a group. Children often gain these skills by watching **role models**.

Key terms

Hand–eye coordination – where eyes and hands work together to manage a task.

Fine manipulative movements – intricate movements of the hands, showing concentration and skill.

Tripod grasp – a pencil hold where the finger and thumb hold the pencil, supported by the middle finger.

Discussion point

In pairs, discuss what you have done so far today. Which of these cognitive skills have you used?

- Planning – e.g. setting an alarm, working out a journey, meeting up with a friend.
- Colour – e.g. working out what to wear, choosing clothes that go together.
- Number – e.g. buying something at a shop.
- Memory – e.g. having remembered something you were told.

Key terms

Perception – the ability to become aware of something by using the senses.

Self-concept – how we view ourselves.

Self-esteem – how much we value ourselves.

Role models – people from whom children copy skills and attitudes.

Just checking

1 How is children's growth measured?
2 What factors might affect children's growth?
3 What are the five areas of development?
4 What is meant by 'gross motor movement'?
5 What is meant by 'cognitive development'?

Assessment practice 1.1

Complete the table by identifying which areas of development and skills are used in these tasks. Give reasons for your answer. The first one has been done for you.

Reading a book	*Communication and language – reading to work out what has been written.*
	Physical development – hand–eye coordination to turn the page.
Playing noughts and crosses	
Picking up and throwing a ball	
Making a sandcastle	

▶ Links between areas of development

Introduction

While it is usual to look separately at each of the areas of development, it is also important to understand that they work together. Think about holding and reading a book. Does this require skills from more than one area of development? Think of two other everyday activities that require a range of skills.

In this section we look at the specific links between the different areas of development. It is important to think about what it would be like for a child if there was a delay or difficulty in one area.

Communication and language development

Figure 1.3 shows how language development is key to many other areas of development.

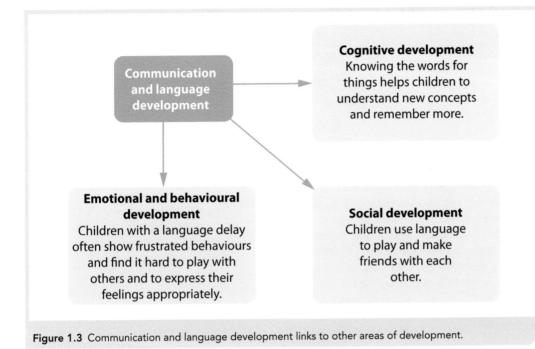

? Did you know?

Children who have communication and language delay are more likely to be excluded from nurseries and schools. This is because it affects their behaviour.

Figure 1.3 Communication and language development links to other areas of development.

Physical development

It would be easy to imagine that physical development would just be about running around or holding things. But being able to move your body, or to touch and hold things, actually makes a difference to children's learning.

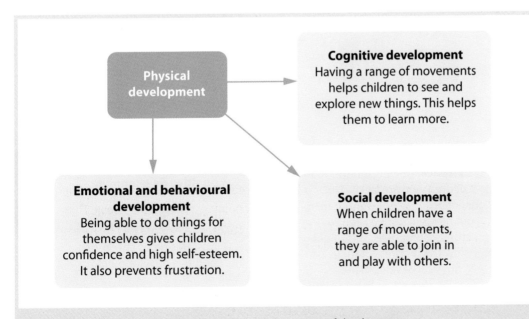

Remember

Physical development is divided into gross motor and fine motor skills. Can you remember the difference between these?

Figure 1.4 Physical development has several other links to areas of development.

Cognitive development

Cognitive development covers the skills that we need to think, remember and take in and also use information. There are many links between cognitive development and other areas.

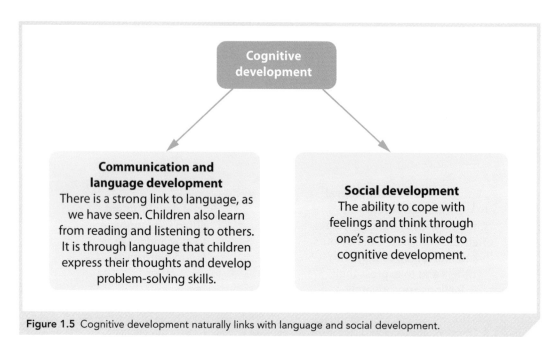

Figure 1.5 Cognitive development naturally links with language and social development.

Emotional and behavioural development

How secure and confident children feel can make a difference to other areas of development.

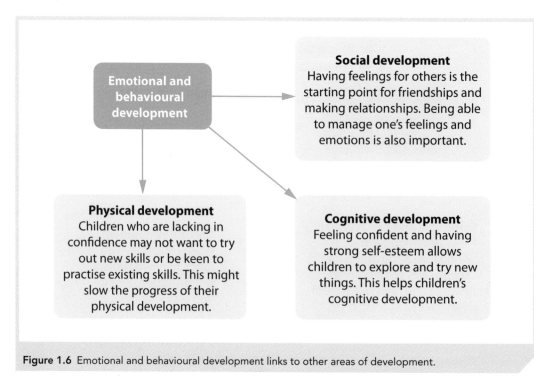

Figure 1.6 Emotional and behavioural development links to other areas of development.

Case study

Lucien is 4 years old. He is not very confident and prefers his parents to do things for him. For example, he lets his parents take off his coat in the morning because he says that he can't do it. When faced with new activities, he waits for an adult to come and help him. He is quite unsure of doing anything that is different. Staff at the nursery are keen to find ways of increasing his confidence as they feel his lack of confidence is affecting his development.

1 Give an example of how Lucien's lack of confidence could be affecting his physical development.

2 Explain how Lucien may be missing out on some aspects of cognitive development.

Social development

If children enjoy being with others and learning how to play, they can gain many other skills from other areas of development.

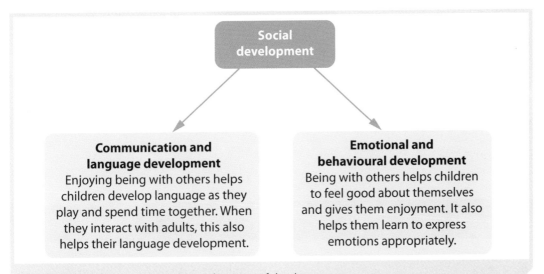

Social development

Communication and language development
Enjoying being with others helps children develop language as they play and spend time together. When they interact with adults, this also helps their language development.

Emotional and behavioural development
Being with others helps children to feel good about themselves and gives them enjoyment. It also helps them learn to express emotions appropriately.

Figure 1.7 Social development links to other areas of development.

These children are both good communicators. How is this helping other areas of their development?

Just checking

1 Can you give an example of how a language delay may cause problems with a child's social development?

2 How does physical development affect a child's learning?

3 Which two areas of development are important in helping a child learn to read and write?

4 Why is children's emotional development important in relation to the development of friendships?

5 Why is it important for adults to know that areas of development relate to each other?

Assessment practice 1.2

You will need to explain how one area of development can be affected by the delay of another.

For each of the five areas of development, give an example of how it might be affected by an aspect of another area of development. An example of how physical development can be affected by emotional development has been done for you.

1 Physical development *can be affected by emotional development – if children are not confident, they might not try out new skills.*

2 Cognitive development

3 Language development

4 Social development

5 Emotional development

▶ Characteristics of development

Introduction

It is helpful to know what most children do at different ages. In this section we will look at what most children will do at different points in their childhood. Of course, every child is different, but many children follow the same pattern.

Discussion point

In pairs, see if you can guess at what age most children say their first words.

▶ Sequences of development

Early years professionals need to know the usual patterns and characteristics of the five areas of development (physical, cognitive, communication and language, emotional and social). In particular, they should consider whether or not children are meeting the milestones associated with their age group. It is important, though, to remember that milestones and characteristics of development can only be a guide. As we have seen earlier, children's development is affected by a wide range of factors. This means that some children are always quicker than others to reach some of the milestones. It also means that some children reach the milestones in one area of development, but not in another area.

Interestingly, when we look at the milestones or characteristics of different age groups, we will see that, quite often, certain milestones have to be reached before others can be achieved. Children will have to walk before they can run or know words before they can say or sign them. This means that, quite often, there are sequences within areas of development. Knowing these sequences is important because it helps early years practitioners plan to provide the right types of resources and activities.

Activity 1.1

Look at the images in Figure 1.8. Using the information in Table 1.2, work out the usual sequence in which babies learn to walk.

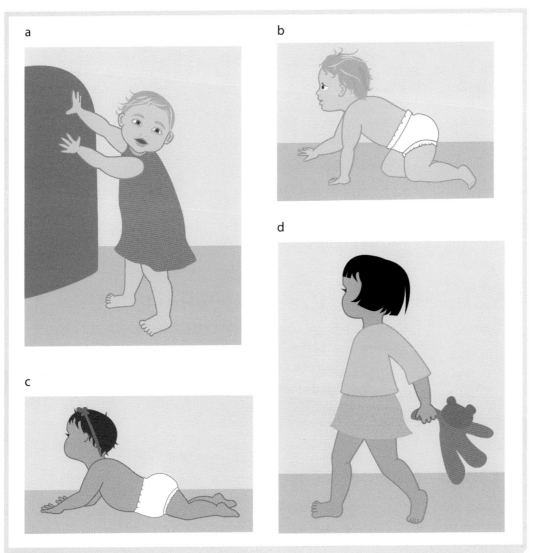

a

b

d

c

Figure 1.8 In what order should these images appear?

Birth up to 12 months

In the first year of life babies show not only amazing growth, but also development. It is probably nature's way of helping them to survive. Babies learn to move and also to communicate. They soon work out who they can rely on for love and attention.

Physical development

Development in the first year is fast. Babies are born pretty much helpless. They rely on some **reflexes** in order to survive. These include the reflex to suck and find food, which is called **rooting**. Babies also grasp tightly to things and respond to sudden sounds with a **startle reflex** by flinging out their arms. Babies cannot control these reflexes. Over time, the reflexes disappear and babies instead learn to control their movements. This control begins with their head. Next they learn whole arm and leg movements until finally they develop some hand–eye coordination.

Key terms

Reflexes – instinctive movements in babies, including startle, sucking, rooting and grasping.

Rooting – instinctive movement that helps babies to find the breast or the bottle's teat.

Startle reflex – instinctive movement when babies fling out their arms in response to sudden sounds or movements.

Table 1.2 Physical development – gross motor movement (birth up to 12 months).

1 month	• Moves head from side to side.
3 months	• Can lift head and chest up when lying on stomach. • When lying on back or being held, can bring hands together.
6 months	• When lying on back, can roll over to front.
9 months	• Can sit up unsupported. • Is likely to be mobile by crawling, rolling or shuffling. • Is starting to pull up to a standing position and may begin to walk by holding on to furniture.
12 months	• Can pull up to a standing position easily. • May be standing alone and walking by holding on to furniture.

Table 1.3 Physical development – fine motor movement (birth up to 12 months).

1 month	• Range of reflexes appear, including swallowing and breathing, which will be permanent. Others are temporary and will disappear over the next few months. • Will grasp things that are put into their hands as a reflex action.
3 months	• Is interested in watching their hands. • Can hold a rattle for a few seconds.
6 months	• Can reach out for a small toy and move it from one hand to another.

9 months	• Can grab things using their **index finger** and thumb. This is called a **pincer grasp**. • Can deliberately drop things, such as a spoon.

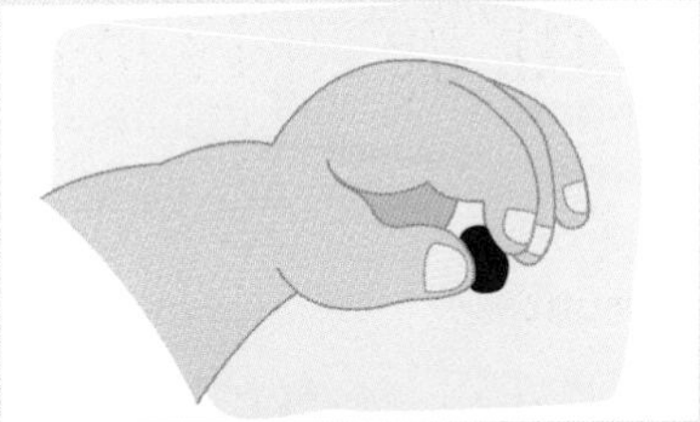

Key terms

Index finger – the finger next to the thumb.

Pincer grasp – using finger and thumb to hold a small item as if pinching.

Figure 1.9 The pincer grasp.

12 months	• Can pick up very small things using a pincer grasp. • Points to objects using index finger.

Cognitive development

In the first year babies are learning about their new world. Their brains are taking in a lot of information that has to be processed. Some experts think that this is why they need to sleep so much.

Table 1.4 Cognitive development (birth up to 12 months).

1 month	'Freezes' on hearing a soft sound, such as tune from a cot mobile.
3 months	• Is more alert. • Will follow movements of objects if they are close by. • Recognises parts of familiar routines, for example, becoming excited on hearing the sound of water for a bath.
6 months	• Explores objects by handling them and **mouthing** them. • Recognises voices.
9 months	• At 8 or 9 months begins to look for things that are put out of sight.
12 months	• Enjoys dropping things such as toys to the ground and watching them fall. • Will repeat actions if pleasurable and interesting. This approach is called **trial and error learning**.

Key terms

Mouthing – putting items in the mouth as a way of playing and as a way of exploring them.

Trial and error learning – learning by trying things out and repeating if successful.

Communication and language development

In the first year babies are trying to tune into the sounds that they are hearing. They need to distinguish between human voices and other sounds. They also need to learn what words actually mean. Babies also make sounds in their first year. By the end of the first year, these sound almost like words.

Table 1.5 Communication and language development (birth up to 12 months).

1 month	• Turns head when hearing a familiar adult voice. • At 6 weeks starts to make cooing sounds.
3 months	• Smiles on hearing a familiar voice.
6 months	• Makes short babbling sounds such as 'ba' and 'pa'.
9 months	• Understands the word 'no'. • Starts to make strings of babbling such as 'dadadadada'.
12 months	• Smiles or shows signs of recognising own name and follows very simple instructions such as 'Where's Daddy?'

Emotional and social development

In the first year of life children's emotional and social development are so closely linked that it is hard to write about them separately. Very early on, babies look at faces and eyes. They also like to be held. For the first few months, babies will smile and enjoy being held by anyone. This gives rise to the term **indiscriminate attachments**, which means that babies appear happy to be around anyone. But from about 7 months or so they start to actively want to be with the important people in their lives, such as their parents. The term **specific attachments** is used to describe these clear preferences.

Table 1.6 Emotional and social development (birth up to 12 months).

1 month	• Stares at human faces with interest. • Wants to be held.
6 weeks	• Starts to smile and respond to smiles.
3 months	• Enjoys being held. • Shows indiscriminate attachments.
6 months	• Can recognise emotions in others, for example, angry gestures and voice tones, and responds to these.

7–8 months	• The first signs of specific attachment are shown by:
	  ▪ crying if held by people they do not know
	  ▪ showing that they care for the key people or **primary carers** in their lives by smiling, wanting to be held by them and becoming distressed if they cannot see them.

8 months	• Specific attachments demonstrated by reactions of babies when they see their primary carers. • **Separation anxiety** is noticeable as babies may cry and become distressed when left alone or in the presence of people they do not know. • Copies gestures and actions of others and enjoys doing so, for example, clapping hands.

Key terms

Indiscriminate attachments – where babies show affection and can be cuddled by people they do not know.

Specific attachments – where babies and young children show affection and can be cuddled or reassured only by their primary carers.

Primary carers – people who have a significant role in a child's life – often, but not always, the child's parents.

Separation anxiety – panic and distress shown when a child cannot see or be with their parents or people they are emotionally close to.

▶ 12 months up to 3 years

In these two years development continues to be rapid. While physical development continues at a steady pace, the really big change is in children's communication and language skills. They go from just babbling at 12 months through to talking in complete sentences at 3 years. It is an incredible journey and one that affects many other areas of their development, as we will see.

Physical development

Babies usually gain mobility in this period and learn to walk. They also learn to coordinate their movements, which allows them to do more complex things, such as bend down and pick up a small object quickly. Moving out of nappies is another big change for children. The timing of this varies. Some children do this before they are 2 years old, but most are between 2 and 3 years.

A baby showing indiscriminate attachment is happy to be cuddled by someone they do not know.

Table 1.7 Physical development – gross motor movement (12 months up to 3 years).

15 months	• Can crawl upstairs. • Can stand and may be walking either hesitantly or holding on to furniture.
18 months	• Can walk without any help. • Can walk upstairs holding on to a rail or an adult's hand. • Can squat down to pick up toys or to look at something of interest.
2 years	• Can run. • Enjoys climbing and may climb on to furniture, such as chairs or low tables. • Can use a sit-and-ride toy and move using feet.
2½ years	• Can kick a large ball. • Can jump with two feet from a low step.
3 years	• Can run forwards and backwards. • Can steer and pedal a tricycle. • Walks upstairs using alternate feet for each step. • Can aim and throw a large ball.

? Did you know?

From around 8 months until they are at least 3 years old, children begin to show separation anxiety. They may cry when they cannot see their parents or someone who is familiar. Or they may cling to their parent when a stranger approaches them. Early years settings help to prevent separation anxiety in children by giving them time to settle in and by making sure that they get to know their key person.

Key term

Key person – an adult who develops a strong, consistent relationship with a child and their family to ensure that a child's emotional needs are met.

Key terms

Palmar grasp – wrapping the whole hand around an object to make a movement (see Figure 1.10).

Hand preference – the hand that is most often used for tasks requiring hand–eye coordination and which will become the hand used for writing.

Table 1.8 Physical development – fine motor movement (12 months up to 3 years).

15 months	• Uses a pincer grasp to pick up small objects accurately. • Holds crayons by wrapping the holding hand around them in a **palmar grasp**.

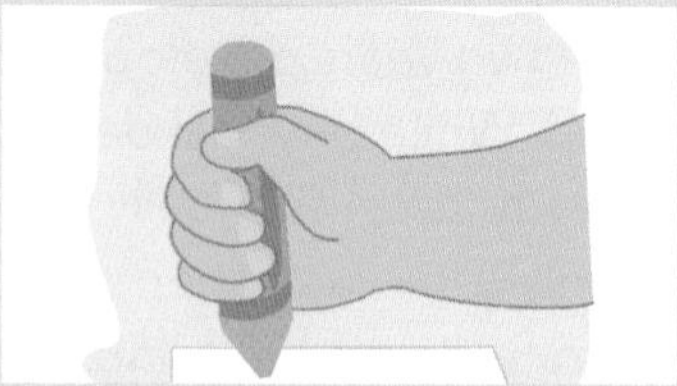

Figure 1.10 The palmar grasp.

18 months	• Has enough hand–eye coordination to build a tower of three bricks. • Can feed self easily with a spoon. • Enjoys scribbling with a crayon.
2 years	• Has sufficient control to draw dots and circles with a crayon. • Can put on shoes and fasten them, but only if they have Velcro®.
2½ years	• **Hand preference** is starting to be seen. • Can pull down items of clothing such as trousers and pants. • Is starting to hold pencils and crayons using a tripod grasp.

Figure 1.11 The tripod grasp.

3 years	• Tripod grasp is used when holding pens and crayons. • Hand preference is established.

Cognitive development

During these two years children are keen to explore and learn more about their world. They start to show that they remember things. Their cognitive development is closely linked to their developing language skills.

Table 1.9 Cognitive development (12 months up to 3 years).

15 months	• Is interested in the sight and sound of objects and is keen to explore. • May still be exploring by putting objects in the mouth, although with less frequency than before.
18 months	• Is very curious and constantly explores objects and how things work. • Remembers where objects that are used often belong, for example, will get spoon from a drawer or put toy back in a toy box.

continued

Table 1.9 continued

2 years	• Recognises self in a mirror and knows that this is not another child! • Can remember things that have happened in the past and shows this by remembering actions, skills, toys and people.
2½ years	• Can point to a photograph of self. • Can complete a simple puzzle with some help.
3 years	• Is starting to understand the difference between past and present. • Can complete a puzzle with 12 pieces.

Jigsaw puzzles are a way of observing children's problem-solving skills.

Communication and language development

This is a period of rapid development in terms of language and communication. Babies who were babbling now start to say the odd word in among the babbling. At 18 months they start saying a few words. Between the ages of 2 and 3, children learn and start to say several new words each week! They also start to put words together into sentences. By 3 years, most children love to chatter.

Table 1.10 Communication and language development (12 months up to 3 years).

15 months	• Communicates by pointing and also vocalises, often by babbling. • Has up to six words.
18 months	• Many children will have around 15 words. Some will have more than this. • Can communicate their wishes using words and gestures. • Understands simple requests, such as 'Get your shoes.'
2 years	• Most children have 50 words. Some children will have more. • Words are just starting to be joined together in two-word sentences, such as 'Ball gone.' • Enjoys looking at books.
2½ years	• Likely to have up to 200 words. Some children will have more. • Uses simple sentences. • Asks simple questions, such as 'What's this?' • Uses **personal pronouns**, **negatives** and **plurals**, for example, 'I don't want bricks.'
3 years	• Speech is clear to anyone who does not know the child well. • Enjoys books and turns pages.

Key terms

Personal pronouns – words such as 'it', 'she', 'he' and 'they' which replace someone's name.

Negatives – a way in speaking and in writing of saying that something is not the case or is not present. This is achieved in several ways, including words such as 'not', 'no one' and 'nothing'.

Plurals – a way in speaking and in writing of communicating that there is more than one object or person. This is usually achieved by adding an 's' to a word, e.g. 'dogs'.

This 2 year old is unsure of strangers. What does this clinginess show?

Emotional and social development

While children's communication and language skills are developing, their emotional and social development is coming along at a much slower pace. This will change once their speech is nearly fluent. In this period children like to be near the people they most care about. They can become very distressed and show separation anxiety if they are not with them. They are often unsure of strangers approaching them and may hide or cling to their familiar adult.

Children are often interested in watching other children, but not until 3 years will they have the social skills to play with them.

Table 1.11 Emotional and social development (12 months up to 3 years).

18 months	• Plays alone but enjoys being near adults, brothers and sisters and other children. • Insists on immediate attention. • Can copy adult actions, for example, throwing a ball.
2 years	• Cannot wait for needs to be met and so tantrums are common. • Can sometimes be distracted from having a tantrum. • Plays in parallel with other children, but not able to share toys.
2½ years	• Plays alongside other children and often watches or copies their actions (onlooker play). • Depends heavily on adults and wants their attention. • Jealous of other children gaining adults' attention. • Responds well to adult attention and praise. • Likely to have tantrums if cannot have own way or get what they have seen.
3 years	• Finds it easier to wait. • Starts to take turns and share with other children. • Enjoys playing with other children. • Will comfort other children in distress.

Just checking

See if you can say whether these statements are 'true' or 'false':

1　Many children aged 2½ years will have temper tantrums.

2　Most babies say their first words at 10 months.

3　It is usual for children from 8 months to cry if they are left with someone they do not know.

4　At 2 years most children are using 50 words.

5　Most babies are walking by 10 months.

6　At 18 months most children can hold a pencil using a tripod grasp.

▶ 3 years up to 5 years

During these years there are a lot of changes in children's social and emotional development. They start to make friends with other children and are able to enjoy being with adults other than their parents. There are changes also in their cognitive development as they start to use their language skills to find out and think about things. Their physical growth and development continues but now at a relatively slow pace.

Physical development

The key change that we see in children aged 3 to 5 is their increasing level of skill in both gross and fine motor development. They start to be able to talk as they pedal or throw. They also start to use their hands to manage tools such as scissors or knives and forks. As some of this development is quite slow, it is harder to separate it into individual months or years. Development from now on also depends on the opportunities that children have to practise movements and skills.

Table 1.12 Physical development – gross motor movement (3 years up to 5 years).

3–4 years	• Can hop on one foot.
	• Can walk along a line.
	• Can aim and throw a ball fairly accurately.
	• Can kick a ball with some force.
	• Can ride a tricycle using pedals and steer it accurately.
4–5 years	• Can run and avoid obstacles.
	• Can skip with a rope (often closer to 5 years).
	• Can throw a large ball to a partner and catch it.

Table 1.13 Physical development – fine motor movement (3 years up to 5 years).

3–4 years	• Can button and unbutton clothes.
	• Uses scissors to cut out simple shapes.
	• Can draw a person with a head, trunk and legs.
	• Eats with a knife and fork.
	• Can thread beads to make a necklace.
4–5 years	• Can form letters.
	• Writes own name.
	• Colours in pictures.

Cognitive development

In these two years children learn to count, start to put things in order and learn concepts such as time, colour and shape. Children's cognitive development depends on adults pointing things out to them and also on whether children have sufficient skills in language to understand the new concepts.

Table 1.14 Cognitive development (3 years up to 5 years).

3–4 years	• Can recognise and name primary colours – blue, red and yellow. • Understands what is meant by 'more'. • Can tell whether an object is heavy or light. • Arranges objects into categories. • Makes connections between people and events.
4–5 years	• Can count accurately up to 10. • Can add two sets of objects together. • Can match equal sets of objects, for example, which two boxes have the same number of beakers. • Can understand the need for rules. • Names times of day associated with different everyday activities, for example, bedtime is at night.

Communication and language development

In these two years children's language becomes fluent, and this is important as talk is a key way in which children will learn. Children will still make some grammatical mistakes, but these will become fewer. Children's communication and language skills help them play with others. They also learn to use language to argue back and to squabble!

Table 1.15 Communication and language development (3 years up to 5 years).

3–4 years	• Speech can be easily understood, although some words may not be pronounced correctly, for example, 'wabbit' instead of 'rabbit'. • Uses questions to gain attention, but also out of genuine interest, especially 'why', 'what' and 'how'. • Fluent speech at 4 years (with some speech immaturities).
4–5 years	• Can count accurately up to 10. • Uses complex sentences with words such as 'because'. • Can talk about what has happened and what might happen. • Uses language to argue and to answer back.

Emotional and social development

Having friends becomes very important in this age range, and this is linked to improved social skills. Children are also learning to express and control their emotions. They have fewer tantrums and angry outbursts unless they are tired. Children are also happier to be separated from their primary carer (usually a parent) if they know the adult they are left with.

Table 1.16 Emotional and social development (3 years up to 5 years).

3–4 years	• Can cope with separation from primary carer when they are with someone they know.
	• Begins to play cooperatively and enjoys playing with others.
	• Shows clear friendship preferences.
4–5 years	• Can work out what others may be thinking – this helps them to negotiate with others.
	• Able to understand the need for rules, although they may not always follow them!
	• Close friendships develop, and children may be sad if their friend is not there.
	• Behaviour is mostly cooperative.
	• Separates more easily from parents.

These children are becoming friends. How can close friendships help a child's emotional and social development?

Assessment practice 1.3

For each area of development, write **four** ways in which children's skills at the age of 4 years will differ from when they were 2 years old. One example has been given.

Physical development

1 *Can now hold a pencil using a tripod grasp.*

Feedback on Student 1

This learner has provided only one point about children's emotional development at this age. It is also not detailed enough to be accurate. The student has given two examples of how adults might support social development, but the examples given are not correct for the age and stage of this child and shows that the student does not have a good grasp of child development. The learner has not explained how their suggestions would support the social development.

Student 2's answer

Most children at 2½ years are interested in other children. They can play alongside them. They also enjoy watching other children play. They want to spend time with adults and they can be jealous if other children take up an adult's time.

The adults at Jamie's nursery can help his social development by organising games where pairs of children with an adult can play together. This will help Jamie and the other children to enjoy each other's company and will help them learn to take turns. The adults can also provide opportunities for Jamie to enjoy being with others at mealtimes. They could encourage the children to pass plates of food around or help set the table. This would help Jamie and the other children to learn to share and think of others.

Feedback on Student 2

This student has correctly identified and described the stage of emotional development associated with this age. The suggestions chosen to illustrate how Jamie's development could be supported are age and stage appropriate. For each suggestion, an explanation of the social skills that it would develop has been provided.

▶ Assess yourself

Question 1

By what age are most children talking fluently? [1]

| A | 18 months | | C | 4 years |
| B | 3 years | | D | 5 years |

Question 3

What is meant by the term 'cognitive development'? Give an example of a cognitive skill. Describe two ways in which adults might support children's cognitive development. [4]

Question 2

What do you understand by the term 'transition'? [2]

Introduction

If you visit any nursery or school, you are bound to find children playing. This is because play is seen as a vital way to support children's development. Early years settings plan a range of play opportunities and activities that will help children to learn. In this unit you will learn about how play can promote children's development. You will also learn about the type of play opportunities that early years settings provide both for babies and young children. During this unit you will also find out that there are many ways in which play can be structured.

Assessment: This unit will be assessed through a series of assignments set by your teacher/tutor.

Learning aims

In this unit you will:

A understand how play promotes children's development in early years settings

B understand how different play opportunities promote children's development

C understand how play is structured in early years settings to promote children's development.

I had no idea how important play was before I did this unit. Now I look at children playing and think about how it is benefiting them.

Tomi, *17-year-old early years student*

Promoting Children's Development Through Play

2

BTEC
Assessment Zone

This table shows what you must do in order to achieve a **Pass**, **Merit** or **Distinction** grade, and where you can find activities in this book to help you.

Assessment criteria			
Level 1	**Level 2 Pass**	**Level 2 Merit**	**Level 2 Distinction**
Learning aim A: Understand how play promotes children's development in early years settings			
1A.1 Identify two ways in which children play at each age range.	**2A.P1** English Describe how children play at each age range, using appropriate examples. **See Assessment activity 2.1, page 53**	**2A.M1** English Explain the importance of the support provided by adults in early years settings for children's play at each age range. **See Assessment activity 2.1, page 53**	**2A.D1** English Assess the suitability of the support provided by adults for children in an early years setting using a case study. **See Assessment activity 2.1, page 53**
1A.2 Identify two ways in which adults in early years settings support the play of children in each age range.	**2A.P2** English Describe how adults in early years settings support children's play at each age range, using appropriate examples. **See Assessment activity 2.1, page 53**		
Learning aim B: Understand how different play opportunities promote children's development			
1B.3 Identify play opportunities for each age range and the development that will be promoted.	**2B.P3** Maths Describe play opportunities for each age range and how development will be promoted, using appropriate examples. **See Assessment activity 2.2, page 62**	**2B.M2** Maths Explain how two selected play opportunities for each age range promote different areas of child development. **See Assessment activity 2.2, page 62**	**2B.D2** Assess the value of two selected play opportunities on all areas of a child's development. **See Assessment activity 2.2, ppage 62**
Learning aim C: Understand how play is structured in early years settings to promote children's development			
1C.4 Outline how early years settings structure play in different ways to promote children's development.	**2C.P4** Describe how early years settings structure play in different ways to promote children's development, using appropriate examples. **See Assessment activity 2.3, page 68**	**2C.M3** Discuss the extent to which the way play is structured in an early years setting may benefit children's development. **See Assessment activity 2.3, page 68**	**2C.D3** Assess the effect on a child's development of the way play is structured in an early years setting, using a case study. **See Assessment activity 2.3, page 68**

English Opportunity to practise English skills

Maths Opportunity to practise mathematical skills

How you will be assessed

This unit will be assessed by a series of internally set tasks provided by your teacher/tutor. Your evidence for this unit will be collected and stored in a portfolio, together with any observation records or witness statements. Throughout this unit you will find assessment practice activities that will help you work towards your assessment. Completing these activities will not mean that you have achieved a particular grade, but you will have carried out useful research or preparation that will be relevant when it comes to your final assignment.

The assignments set by your teacher will consist of a number of tasks designed to meet the criteria in the table. This is likely to consist of written assignments and may include activities such as producing:

- a leaflet or chart to show a manager that you understand how children play at different ages and the ways in which adults can support this play
- an information file for staff about play opportunities for children from birth to 8 years
- a leaflet, chart or other information for parents to help them understand the different ways in which play can be structured.

Gower College Swansea
Library
Coleg Gŵyr Abertawe
Llyrfgell

▶ Play at different ages and stages of development

Introduction

Play is something that all children seem to enjoy doing. During play children are practising skills and movements. This supports their development. This is why early years settings use play as a key way to help children learn and develop.

Discussion point 💬

In pairs, discuss the following questions:

- What type of games did you play as a child?
- Did these change as you grew up?

Key term 🔒

Mouthing – putting items in the mouth as a way of playing and as a way of exploring them.

If you were to watch two children of different ages, you would notice that their play is quite different. This is because, as children grow and develop, their play changes. A good example is the way in which older children often play games, such as football, that require coordination and skills. Children's language development also changes their play. From around 2 years onwards you are likely to see that children enjoy role play, and with growing social skills most children from around 3 years want to play with others.

The change in children's development and their play means that they will have different needs when it comes to play. Adults working with children have to recognise the different ways in which children play at different ages and ensure that children are sufficiently challenged.

▶ How children play from birth up to 2 years

There are several key features about this age range.

This baby is playing and exploring by mouthing.

Reliance on adults

Firstly babies and toddlers are very reliant on adults. They like adults to play simple games with them. They also like to stay physically close to adults. Toddlers will often move their toys to be next to a familiar adult. Older babies and toddlers also enjoy watching older children play.

Moving and touching

Another characteristic of this age group is the way that they enjoy touching things using their hands and, up until 18 months, their mouth. When babies put things in their mouth, this is called **mouthing**.

Once babies are mobile, there is no stopping them! They move to touch, open and hold new items. They want to explore their surrounding environment.

Repeating play

Interestingly, when babies and toddlers have found play that they enjoy, they want to repeat it over and over again, for example, knocking down towers of blocks, watching a jack-in-the-box pop up or pushing toys cars down a slope.

▶ How children play from 2 up to 5 years

As children move from babyhood to childhood, their play changes.

Being with other children

In the next phase of play we see that children start to be very interested in being with other children. At first they play side by side, but from around 3 years children start to play together. They start to talk to each other, take turns and begin to share toys and resources. This is called **cooperative play**. By 4 years most children are very good at playing with other children.

More complex play

Children's play also changes because their physical skills have developed. Some of their play now involves moving. They enjoy climbing, balancing and also throwing and kicking balls. From around 4 years this becomes more complex and organised.

Talk during play

The other key aspect of development that affects children's play is language. From 2 years children talk as they are playing. At first 2 year olds talk by themselves and some of what they say may not be easy to understand. As speech becomes clearer, they use language increasingly during imaginative play and construction play.

Adult supervision and support

Even if children are playing well together, they still need the support of adults. They like showing adults what they are doing to gain encouragement and also reassurance. Adults are also needed to supervise children and keep them safe.

▶ How children play from 5 up to 8 years

By the time children are around 5 years, their play changes to become more complex and less dependent on adult help.

Becoming more independent

Children in this age range are becoming increasingly independent. They enjoy making decisions about what and who they want to play with. They often can play for long periods without needing adult help. Adults do need to keep an eye on what they are doing, though, to make sure that they are safe.

Discussion point

Toys that are made and sold for babies must not have any small parts. Discuss with a partner why this is important, given the way that babies are likely to play.

Key term

Cooperative play – taking part in play with other children.

Remember

Look back at Unit 1. Can you see the link between children's play and their social development?

Older children play without the support of an adult.

Making up rules

A feature of this age is that they enjoy making up rules to make their play more challenging. They may, for example, decide that you have to roll a dice or have a password before coming into a den. Some rules may also include who can and cannot join the play. This type of rule might need to be challenged by adults!

Increasingly complex play

As well as play becoming more challenging in terms of rules, it also becomes more complex in several ways. Children may play with smaller, intricate toys such as Lego©Technic™. Outdoor play such as obstacle courses or games involving a ball may require a higher level of skill.

Case study

Miriam, Stephan, Mark and Evan are great friends. They are in their second year at school. They cannot wait to go out and play every break and lunchtime. They have favourite games and at the moment their play is influenced by a television game show. There are other groups of children also playing a similar version of the same game. Another child comes and asks if he can join in. The children decide that he can and start to explain the rules. The game requires children to run with a ball, throw it to a partner and then get back to a bench without being caught. The game is very exciting and occasionally an adult has to intervene to stop it from becoming unsafe.

1 Explain why their play is typical of their age.

2 Give two reasons why adults might have to intervene in this type of play.

3 Identify the links between the children's social development and the way that they play.

Just checking

1 Can you think of two ways in which a baby might play?

2 Why is it important to recognise the play needs of different ages of children?

3 Can you think of two features of children's play at 4 years old?

4 Can you think of two examples of how children aged 5–8 might play?

5 Why is play thought to be good for children's overall development?

▶ How and why adults support children's play

Introduction

Adults in early years settings support children's play. In this section you will learn about what they do to support play and why it is important.

Adults in early years settings plan carefully for children's play. They do this based on children's ages. They also think about children's interests. To support some children's development, they choose particular games or equipment. Adults also make sure that what is on offer for children links to the early years curriculum.

▶ Supporting play from birth up to 2 years

Babies and toddlers need adults to play with them.

Enjoyable play

Some of the earliest games with babies are rhymes such as 'Humpty Dumpty' or 'Round and Round the Garden'. Adults have to make games fun so that children learn that playing with others is enjoyable.

Safe play

Adults also have to choose toys and resources that are safe. Babies explore things by putting them in the mouth. If items are not carefully chosen, the baby can choke. Items also need to be easily cleaned.

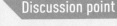

Discussion point

In pairs, make a list of ways in which you think adults might support children's play. At the end of the topic, compare your list with what you have learned.

Did you know?

In the UK, each of the home countries has its own curriculum framework. In England the framework is called the Early Years Foundation Stage. It covers birth to 5 years and, by law, must be followed in every early years setting.

Why is this rattle safe for the baby?

Interesting play

Babies and toddlers are new to play. This means that adults help them by showing and holding out things that might interest them, such as rattles, puppets and shakers.

Adult help with play

Adults also need to help children know what to do with certain toys, such as a pop-up toy or a peg and hammer toy. Adults can show children what to do, for example, they may build a tower of blocks or drop a shape into the shape sorter.

▶ Supporting play from 2 up to 5 years

At this stage of development most children are able to become slightly more independent, especially from around 3 years. In this phase adults have to encourage them in cooperative play and their growing independence.

Encouraging independence

Children from 2 years are starting to enjoy play. They still have skills to learn and adults can help them. Adults help children by encouraging them to choose toys and resources. There are many ways of doing this. Adults can make sure that they put resources at the right height for children so they can reach them. They can ask children what they would like to play with or, in the case of younger children, show them items and how they work.

Supervising children

Adults also help children to stay safe. They supervise children carefully. They need to keep an eye out for children who are becoming frustrated or angry with each other, as well as noticing when play is becoming boisterous or potentially unsafe. Children are still learning about how to play cooperatively and this can mean that they squabble and argue. Adults have to supervise and sometimes intervene. This has to be done in a way that does not make children lose confidence in their ability to play more independently. For example, an adult might go over to children who are squabbling over a toy and state that it can be hard when everyone wants to play with the same thing. The adult could go on to suggest ways of resolving the conflict or, if the children have good language skills, ask them if they know how they might do this.

Case study

A couple of 4 year olds are pretending to play 'pets'. One child is the owner. The other is pretending to be the dog. They are having great fun together. The 'owner' decides that the dog needs to be taken for a walk. She spots a belt in the dressing-up box. She says, 'Look! Come and put your lead on.' The other child sits while the first child starts to tie the belt around her friend's neck. An adult immediately intervenes.

1 Why did the adult intervene?

2 Why is it important to supervise children even when they are playing well?

Joining in play

Adults can also support children's play by joining in with them. This helps younger children to learn to take turns, share equipment and be cooperative. Joining in their play also helps to promote children's language and social skills.

What skills are these children learning?

Setting up new play opportunities

Children are fairly new to play and have plenty to discover. Adults can extend children's play and development by putting out new equipment, interesting resources and setting up areas so that they look attractive. This means that in early years settings you might find that suitable equipment is carefully laid out alongside sensory materials (such as dough and water). On the collage table there is usually a wide range of materials available for children to choose from. By setting up play opportunities attractively, adults find that children are more likely to use them and so learn new skills or concepts. It also helps children to concentrate for longer.

▶ Supporting play from 5 up to 8 years

In this next age group children can play for longer periods and need less adult support. They are likely to play cooperatively most of the time and they understand the need to take turns.

Supervision

Supervision remains important. Adults need to supervise children by keeping an eye on them, but in ways that are more discreet. This approach is important as children are more **self-conscious** and so find it harder to be imaginative when adults are looking at them. If the adult takes a step back, this will help children to sort out for themselves how to take turns, and this approach helps children to gain confidence.

Key term

Self-conscious – being aware of oneself and of what others might think about you.

Teaching games

While at times adults will take a step back, there are times when adults will actively teach children to play new games to support their logic or mathematical skills. Examples may include noughts and crosses, chess or board games such as snakes and ladders. Once children have been taught these games, they can go on to play them with other children.

Providing more challenging opportunities

Adults can also help children's play by providing more challenging opportunities for physical play. They may put out an obstacle course that requires children to balance or put out a climbing frame that allows children to climb higher. As children become older, adults often organise team games. These develop children's physical skills, but also help children to feel part of a group.

How can team games help children to feel part of a group?

Helping children learn about keeping safe

We have seen that adults keep on supervising children even up to the age of 8. But adults also need to help children learn the skills of keeping themselves safe. They may do this by talking to children before or during play about how they might keep themselves safe, and by asking them if they can identify any possible risks.

Just checking

1 Can you think of two ways in which adults might provide play for babies and children who are under 2 years?

2 Why are children aged 2–5 years encouraged to select resources?

3 Can you think of two examples of ways in which adults might support play for children aged 2–5 years?

4 Why would adults teach children aged 5–8 years to play games such as noughts and crosses?

5 Why is it important that children learn to manage risk?

Assessment activity 2.1

2A.P1 | 2A.P2 | 2A.M1 | 2A.D1

Monty's daycare nursery is about to have an inspection. The manager wants you to look at how adults are supporting children's play. You are to provide feedback to the staff in the form of a presentation.

In the main room, where there are 3 and 4 year olds, you see that there are some children in the home corner. There are not enough things available for them to play with, but the adult in the room has not noticed. The children look bored.

In another part of the room an adult is playing with a small group of children. She is joining in with their play and helping them to take turns.

In the baby room an adult is setting up beakers on the floor and letting a baby knock them down. The baby laughs and the adult smiles. They are having fun.

Outdoors there are some older children in an afterschool club. Some of the children are kicking a ball. The adult is keeping an eye on their safety and at one point talks to them about how to keep their play safe.

In your feedback to the staff you should:

• explain how children's play changes according to their age/stage of development and give examples of this for each of the following ages of children: 0–2 years, 2–5 years and 5–8 years

• for each age/stage, explain what adults should do to support children's play and give some examples of this

• explain the importance of this adult support for each age group

• provide feedback about the strengths and weaknesses of the current adult support being given to children in this setting.

Tips

• Remember that you need to provide information about how play changes and about the adult role in supporting each of the three age ranges. You must also provide examples to back up your information.

• You also need to assess carefully the suitability of adult support. To do this, you need to think about how strong the adult support is and whether this is sufficient.

▶ Play opportunities and how they promote children's development

Introduction

Early years settings provide children with a wide range of play opportunities. This is because different resources and games are good for promoting different areas of development.

Discussion point

Think about an early years setting that you know. In pairs, write down five different toys and resources that you might expect to see.

In this section we look at the different types of play opportunities that are usually provided in early years settings for different ages of children. Each play opportunity helps children to gain certain skills which will support their development (physical, cognitive, language and communication, emotional and social). For children to master skills and concepts, the toys, activities and resources have to be right for their age and stage of development.

▶ Play opportunities from birth up to 2 years

Babies and toddlers need a wide range of play opportunities that allow them to gain physical skills and to explore textures. They also need play opportunities with adults that allow them to learn that play is enjoyable.

Physical play

Key terms

Fine motor movements – small movements usually associated with the hands.

Gross motor movements – large movements of the arms and legs.

Physical play encourages babies and toddlers to move and to learn to coordinate their movements. Play opportunities need to help children's **fine motor movements** and also their **gross motor movements**. Once babies are mobile and they are more coordinated, they need more challenging opportunities.

Activity 2.1

The table shows some of the toys and resources that might be used in physical play to support babies who are not yet mobile and older children. Look at a toy catalogue and see if you can add to the list.

	Toys that support fine motor movements	Toys that support gross motor movements
Non-mobile babies	Rattles Soft toys	Baby gym Baby bouncer
Mobile babies and toddlers	Stacking beakers	Push-and-pull toys Balls

Heuristic play

Heuristic play helps babies and toddlers to discover textures. It also helps babies and toddlers to concentrate and learn about shapes and sizes. This type of play fosters creativity and imagination. With non-mobile babies objects made from natural materials are put out in a form of heuristic play known as **treasure basket play**. The way children play with objects changes as they develop. For example, toddlers begin to spend longer dropping smaller objects into containers. Table 2.1 gives examples of items that might be included in heuristic play and treasure basket play.

Key terms

Heuristic play – play in which children learn from discovering a range of objects.

Treasure basket play – discovery play for babies where all the objects are made from natural materials.

Table 2.1 Treasure basket play and heuristic play.

Treasure basket play	Heuristic play
Items may include: • leather wallet • wooden spoon • metal tea strainer • lavender bag • wooden curtain rings • a fresh lemon • small metal lid • silk scarf.	Items may include: • plastic water bottle • curlers • corks • shells • cardboard tubes • small tins • wooden pegs.

This child is engaged in heuristic play. How are they learning?

Adapting provision to meet individual needs

In order to meet some children's needs, settings will need to adapt their provision. This means that they might need to change the layout, order some new resources or change their routines slightly. There will be many reasons why settings will need to adapt their provision, for example, to help children with mobility needs, dietary needs or any **sensory impairment** they might have.

Keeping children safe

An inclusive environment is also one that ensures that children feel and are kept safe. Staff must be trained to understand the causes of accidents and incidents and know about ways of preventing them.

Establishing routines

An inclusive setting also establishes routines that meet the individual needs of children. These routines include feeding, sleeping, resting, toileting and time spent playing. This is particularly important when it comes to babies and toddlers who may each have their own feeding and sleeping pattern. Establishing these routines links back to working closely with parents and developing a positive relationship with them, as they provide the information needed to establish these routines.

Positive role models

An inclusive setting helps children learn about how to treat and respect others. It also helps children learn that we all have different needs, preferences and ways of living. A key way that children will learn this is by observing how adults behave towards other adults and children. Children who see adults showing interest, respect and kindness towards others are more likely to behave in the same way. Adults who do this are acting as positive role models.

Key term

Sensory impairment – a difficulty with one or more of your senses, for example, your sight, hearing or touch.

This child can learn to identify colours using a special colour chart.

Just checking

1 Why is it important for adults to adopt a non-judgemental attitude?

2 Can you think of two examples of resources that might support inclusive practice?

3 How can a good relationship between a setting and a family help meet a child's needs?

4 Can you think of one reason why early years settings should make necessary adaptions?

5 How might adults act as role models to support inclusive practice?

Assessment activity 3.2   2B.P3 | 2B.M2 | 2B.D2

You have been asked to find out about how inclusive practice can be implemented in early years settings. Children may need inclusive practice if they are shy, or if they are struggling to settle into a new setting. You are to write a report about this. Choose an early years setting to visit or ask someone about how they implement inclusive practice in their setting.

Your report should include:

- ways in which it is possible for early years settings to implement inclusive practice
- how the early years setting that you have learned about implements inclusive practice, and how successful it is in doing this.

Tip

- Try to give examples of how inclusive practice is implemented. These examples should be from the early years setting that you have researched. You should also discuss how successfully the setting is implementing inclusive practice. To do this, think about what they are doing well, as well as how they could improve, making sure you consider all the relevant factors and which are the most important.

Learning aim C   **TOPIC**   **C1**

▶ Empowering children in early years settings

Key term

Empowerment – giving children involvement in decisions that affect them, appropriate to their age and level of understanding.

Introduction

The **empowerment** of children is an important principle in early years settings. Think about the things that you have done for yourself today. Maybe you have chosen what to wear, fed yourself and decided what and when to eat. What would it feel like if someone else always made these choices for you?

Discussion point

In pairs, imagine your day. Now, discuss how it would feel if someone else made a decision about:

- what you wore
- what you ate
- when you ate.

For children to grow into confident, active people, they need to be given opportunities to make choices and gradually to take responsibility for themselves. Settings therefore try to find ways of helping children to make choices or be involved in decisions as part of the everyday running of the setting.

The term empowerment is used to describe this way of working. Adults working with children have to judge carefully how they empower children. Children can only make choices and decisions if they understand the consequences and the different options. The choices they are given must be right for their age and understanding. This means that 2 year olds are not given the option of only eating chocolate at mealtimes!

Why early years settings empower children

Empowering children is seen as an important way of working with children for a variety of reasons.

Legal right

Interestingly, children actually have a right under the United Nations Convention on the Rights of the Child to be informed and consulted about things that will affect their life. It is therefore considered to be good practice to find ways of helping children to make decisions – even small ones – such as choosing what to play with or serving themselves food. It is important to stress that the level of choice and decisions must be right for the age and stage of the child.

Valuing and respecting children

Working in ways that empower children also shows respect for them as human beings. It is a way of showing dignity. Waiting for a baby to be ready before cleaning his face is a way of showing that we value him, even though he is not yet talking or making decisions. In the same way, asking children where and how they would like to say goodbye to their parent is way of valuing their feelings. This, in turn, is a way of showing respect for a child.

Take it further

Many people do not know that children have rights. Find out more about children's rights. Now go to www.pearsonhotlinks.co.uk, search for this title and click on this activity.

Helping children to respect themselves and others

How you are treated as a child affects how you feel about yourself and how you treat others. Children who have been in settings that are empowering learn how to make decisions. This helps them to have confidence in their own judgement, and they can develop self-respect. Children who have also seen the way that adults respect other children by empowering them are more likely to treat others with respect.

How has this child been empowered?

Involving children in decision making

Early years settings also empower children to ensure that their provision works well. Children who have been involved in the choice of play opportunities or in the development of routines are likely to be happy. This helps the setting to run smoothly. Settings that are good at empowering children tend to be happy places.

Case study

Happy Lions staff realised one day that their main 'customers' were really the children. This made them start to think about how they could find ways to make sure their customers' wishes were really met. Some of the staff thought that this would not be possible, as the setting included babies. After some training, they realised that, in all sorts of small ways, even babies could make decisions or be supported to make their wishes clear.

Staff began to notice babies' reactions to toys and activities and used this information to plan. They also made a photo album of resources so that toddlers who were not yet speaking could communicate to staff what they wanted to play with, by pointing. After a few months staff found that children were actually quite good at making decisions. The children also appeared happier.

1 What skills were children gaining from being consulted more?

2 Why might being more involved in decision making help children feel happy?

When children choose for themselves, they are more likely to try out a new skill.

▶ Benefits of empowerment

Early years settings are aware that there are many developmental benefits associated with empowering children.

Emotional development

Children develop a strong sense of self-esteem because they have been involved in decision making and because they feel valued. Empowering children also helps them to manage their own behaviour. This is because, if they have been involved in boundary setting or talking through the expectations for their behaviour, they can understand the reasons behind it.

Physical development

Because children are making decisions about what to play with, they are more likely to try out new skills and practise them. Children also learn about weighing up risk when they have the opportunity to make their own decisions about play.

Social development

As we have already seen, children who feel valued are more likely to show self-respect and to respect and value others. Empowering children also helps them understand the importance of recognising their own feelings and the feelings of others.

Cognitive development

Children are more likely to concentrate and persevere if they have been involved in making decisions about what to do and play with. Concentration is important for learning. Children will also develop logic and thinking skills, as these are required when making decisions.

Just checking

1 What is meant by the term 'empowerment'?
2 Can you think of two reasons why early years settings might seek to empower children?
3 Why might the empowerment of children help their self-esteem?
4 Why might the empowerment of children support their social development?
5 Can you think of a way in which empowerment benefits children's cognitive development?

TOPIC   C2

▶ How adults in early years settings empower children

Introduction

There are many ways in which settings can empower children. Some of these are very small, but still important. It is good practice, for example, for adults to let children put on their own shoes, rather than automatically doing it for them. Can you think why?

The principles of empowerment are fairly simple to understand. They are about giving choice, being respectful and encouraging children to be actively involved in what is happening. Adults working in early years settings need, though, to think about the age and stage of each child, to make sure that children are empowered according to their age and stage of development. Adults also have to find ways of empowering babies and very young children who may not be speaking.

Case study

Harriet is working in an inclusive setting. She has been in the job for just a few weeks and she has been listening to staff members talk about the importance of choice and empowering children. Today she is working with children at the painting table. A 2-year-old child picks up a paint pot and a brush and takes it over to the book corner. The child starts to paint books. Another member of staff intervenes. Afterwards, Harriet is asked why she did not stop the child. She says that it was the child's choice to do this and she wanted to empower the child.

1 Why did the staff member intervene?

2 Explain why empowerment needs to be linked to the age/stage of the child and their understanding of consequences.

▶ Empowering children according to their age

There are many ways in which adults work to empower babies and children in early years settings.

Physical care routines

Physical care routines include dressing, washing, going to the toilet and also nappy changing. Empowering babies and children means helping them to do as much as they can. Even babies can often pull off their socks! With nappy changing, we empower children by letting them hold items or even go and get their clean nappy from the box. Not rushing nappy changes and making them feel as important as possible is also a way of showing respect for the child.

Privacy

As part of the physical care routines, it is important to be aware of the need for privacy when children get a little older. Holding a door slightly ajar, so that a child can sit on the toilet without feeling watched, would be a good example. In the same way, encouraging children to pull up their own underwear, even though they might need help with fastening other garments, helps to show that we respect their privacy.

Mealtimes

Being able to feed yourself is an important stepping stone for children's independence. This begins when children are babies, for example, recognising that a baby has had enough during a feed because she has turned her head away.

It is not good practice, therefore, to force a child to keep eating, although, where there are concerns about food intake, adults might encourage a child to have some more. It is good practice with toddlers and older children to let them serve themselves. This works well, provided that all the food on offer is nutritious. By letting children choose how much food goes on their plate, children also learn to judge their appetite.

How are these children developing their independence?

Child-initiated play

Child-initiated play is provided in all early years settings. By choosing what they wish to play with and how they wish to use resources, children are empowered. Adults might join in this play, but it is the children who initiate it. Children can decide who they want to play with as well. For babies, empowering them in child-initiated play means following their interests. As most babies can point from around 9 or 10 months, they may indicate what it is they wish to play with.

Involving children in planning and gaining feedback

We can ask children who are talking to let us know what they would like to play with or do. This can be incorporated into the planning. Some settings also take photographs of activities so that children who are not yet talking can point to things that they would like to do.

Children can also give feedback about what they like or don't like! Feedback from babies and toddlers can be gained by observing their reactions. Older children might tell us what they think.

Caring for their environment

Empowering children also makes them feel part of the setting. It helps them to feel involved. Most children enjoy helping adults and doing things. This gives them a sense of responsibility. Many settings will encourage children to put out equipment, tidy away and help the adults prepare snacks and drinks. Some settings also encourage children to do a little simple gardening or to put food out for the birds.

Did you know?

Many nurseries and pre-schools have 'snack bars'. These allow children to help themselves to their morning or afternoon snack at a time that suits them. Children serve themselves, although an adult is on hand to check which children have had a drink and to help children if needed. Many settings find this system better than making the children sit down all at once.

Link

Go to *Unit 2: Promoting Children's Development Through Play* where you will find out more information about how child-initiated play is provided in early years settings.

These children have chosen to come to clear the leaves. What skills are they learning?

Just checking

1 Can you think of an example of how to empower a baby as part of their physical care routine?
2 Can you think of two ways in which children might be empowered as part of a setting's toileting routines?
3 How might supporting children to be independent at mealtimes be beneficial?
4 Why might a setting encourage child-initiated play?
5 Why might encouraging children to tidy up support their empowerment?

Assessment activity 3.3

2C.P4 | 2C.P5 | 2C.M3 | 2C.D3

An early years manager has asked you to do a training session for new members of staff. You decide to visit the nursery first. You see that children spend a lot of their time being told what to do by adults. At mealtimes adults serve the children. In the afternoon there is a period when children are able to choose toys and equipment to play with. You also see that children are encouraged to put their own wellingtons and coats on before going outdoors.

In your training session you should cover:

- what is meant by empowerment
- ways in which adults in early years settings can empower children
- why empowerment is considered important for children's overall development.

Tip

- Remember to provide detailed examples of how effective empowerment can benefit children's development. Think about the information that you have about the early years setting and consider how it is empowering children. You can also give examples of what they are doing well, as well as suggestions for improvements.

▶ Why the key person approach is used in early years settings

Introduction

In early years settings a key person system is used. A key person is someone who builds a special relationship with a child so that they feel cared for. This is important as young children can feel quite lost without their parents.

▶ What is a key person?

Babies and young children rely on their parents to meet their emotional needs. When children's parents are not there, they need instead to have someone looking after them who will build a strong relationship with them. Parents also need to know who will be looking out for their child. In early years settings each child will have a key person who takes on this role. Although the term key person is used in this qualification, this role is sometimes referred to as 'key worker'.

Discussion point

In pairs, discuss the following questions:
- Have you ever been somewhere new and someone has looked after you?
- How did this make you feel?

▶ The role of the key person

The key person has several roles.

Develop a special bond with the child

It is the major role of the key person to be able to develop a strong bond with the child. They do not take on the role of being a parent, but more that of a close family member who cares for the child. The bond means that this is an enjoyable relationship for both child and adult.

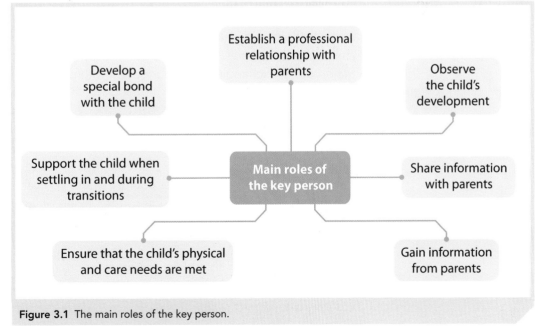

Figure 3.1 The main roles of the key person.

Establish a professional relationship with parents

It is essential that the key person develops a strong relationship with parents or carers quickly. This has to be a professional relationship, although it must be a friendly one. This relationship is important, as information about the needs and development of the child will be shared. Parents can find it hard to leave their child in the care of people who are not family or friends. By establishing a strong bond with the child, as well as with the parents, the key person can make this separation easier.

Observe the child's development

As the key person will spend time with the child and know them well, they will also have a role in the observation of their development. The key person will look at each area of a child's development. In many settings, the key person will also plan activities to support the child's development.

How can you tell that this key person has a special bond with this baby?

Share and gain information

There is a surprising amount of information that must be exchanged in order to meet children's needs and support their development. This includes details of any medical conditions, such as asthma, as well as information on dietary needs or allergies. The setting should be given any other practical information they might need, such as emergency contact details.

Parents should tell the key person about their child's likes and dislikes and about the routines their child is used to. In addition, parents need to know details about their child's care and development when their child is at the setting. The key person has a major role in exchanging this information with parents.

Activity 3.2

We all have different preferences and needs, which may include dietary or medical ones. Children are not always able to explain these to adults. With a friend, imagine that you are in another country where you cannot talk or understand what is happening, but you have an interpreter. None of your belongings are with you. You are in a building with people that you have never met. You will be there for ten hours.

1 What information should your interpreter provide the people with which will help them to meet your needs?

2 Why is it important that these people and your interpreter get on well?

Ensure that the child's physical and care needs are met

By working well with parents, the key person can find out all they need to know about the child's physical and care needs. The key person must ensure that these needs are met while the child is in the setting. They may, for example, personally serve their key child food to ensure that the child's dietary needs are met or they may keep a close eye on a child with asthma during physical activity. As well as being aware of health and dietary needs, the key person must also make sure that children's routine physical care needs are met. A child might need a comforter to help him fall asleep, or a parent might request that the key person uses a barrier cream when changing a nappy.

Support the child when settling in and during transitions

- **Settling in.** The key person plays an essential role in **settling in** the children in their care. A strong relationship with the key person will help children cope when their parents leave. Settling in can take some time, as children will have to get to know their key person and also the setting. Many settings organise a series of visits to help settling in, including a visit to the child's home by their key person.

- **Transitions.** During their lives, children will make many **transitions**. This will include moving to different rooms within a setting, transferring to a different setting or on to a school. Key persons can help children prepare for a transition. They may do this by talking about the changes that are going to be made, reading stories that deal with similar situations or giving children opportunities to talk about their fears. For some transitions, such as the start of school, key persons may also go with their key children on a visit to the new setting.

The key person approach is a statutory requirement

The key person approach is a requirement of early years education and care frameworks in the UK (for example, the Early Years Foundation Stage in England, or the Foundation Phase in Wales). Sometimes the term 'key worker' is used, for example, in Wales. In England it is a statutory requirement, which means that there is a legal requirement for every child who attends an early years setting to be allocated a key person.

Key terms

Settling in – the process by which children become familiar with the setting and their key person.

Transitions – long- or short-term changes that affect the child's life, for example, starting pre-school or changing carer.

Take it further

Find out whether the term 'key person' or 'key worker' is used in settings near to where you live.

Just checking

1 What is meant by the term 'key person'?

2 Why might the key person role support a child's emotional development?

3 Why is it important for key persons to work with children's families?

4 Can you think of two examples of information that might be shared between a key person and a parent?

5 Can you think of two reasons why an early years setting might have a key person system?

How the key person approach supports children's development

Introduction

Children benefit from being with someone who they care about and who nurtures them. Can you think of someone in your childhood with whom you had a strong relationship? What do you feel you gained from being with them?

The key person approach benefits children in a range of ways. It has been shown that children's development can be affected if children do not have a strong bond with another adult when they are not with their parents or primary carers.

Emotional development

One of the main ways in which the key person approach benefits children is in their emotional development. The support that children gain from their key person prevents them from becoming distressed. This is because they have a relationship with the key person and feel nurtured.

The key person also knows the child well and understands how to meet the child's emotional needs. They will, for example, understand when a child is wanting a cuddle or needs their comforter. When children have a key person, they are likely to find future separations easier, for example, starting school, because they are emotionally secure.

How will the emotional connection between this child and her key person help the child's emotional development?

Language development

Children talk to and communicate with people more when they are comfortable with them. When children are benefiting from a strong key person system, they are more likely to want to chat or, in the case of babies, to babble.

As the key person spends quite a lot of time with their key children, they are likely to understand what babies and children are trying to communicate. This is particularly important in the early stages of language development. If children keep trying to communicate and the other person does not understand or acknowledge them, they may stop trying after a while. The key person will also know how best to communicate with the child, as they will know how to encourage the child to respond.

Children's learning

The key person approach is also essential for developing children's skills and overall learning. Children learn more when they enjoy being with an adult that they like and by doing things that interest them. As the key person knows the children's interests, they are more likely to provide opportunities for the child to try new experiences or to explore. They are also likely to provide activities that will really engage the child and help them to develop concentration skills.

Physical development

We have seen earlier that a key person is likely to observe a child and so know a great deal about the child's stage of development. This knowledge is important when planning activities to promote children's physical development because the equipment, activities and resources will be right for their interests and stage of development. Children are also more likely to have a go or practise skills because they enjoy being with their key person.

Social development

In order for children to develop friendships from around the age of 3 years, they need first to have experienced nurturing relationships with adults. The key person approach means that children learn to have trusting relationships beyond their family circle. This teaches them to trust other people. In addition, the key person can help children learn to play with others by playing alongside them. This helps children learn to build relationships with other children.

Just checking

1 How might a key person support the language development of a child?

2 What is the link between children's learning and the role of the key person?

3 How might a key person support children's social development?

4 Can you give an example of how the key person role supports children's learning?

5 Can you think of two examples of how a key person might support a child's physical development?

Assessment activity 3.4

2D.P6 | 2D.P7 | 2D.M4 | 2D.D4

You have been asked to **explain** to a new parent why early year settings use a key person approach. You should cover:

- the reasons why the key person approach is used in early years settings
- the benefits to children's development when the key person approach is used.

You will also need to **evaluate** the contribution a key person makes to a child's development and include specific examples in your response.

Tip

- In order to evaluate the contribution of a key person, you will need to show that you can consider the effects on a particular child's development and link the theory that you have learned about the importance of a key person to practical examples. You will also need to show that you have formed your own conclusions about the effectiveness of the key person approach.

WorkSpace

▶ Lin Chapman

Pre-school supervisor

I have been working at this pre-school for ten years now. I am responsible for the smooth running of the setting. We have many volunteers and work experience students who come here on placement. I try to help them understand the principles behind how we work. It is known as being a happy place.

We pride ourselves on being an inclusive setting. This means looking for ways to make sure that everyone feels that they are welcome, especially families and children, and also that their thoughts, ideas and needs are important to us. As part of this, we spend a lot of time talking and listening not only to families about their needs and ideas, but also to the children themselves.

We want children to feel that they are special and that their ideas count too. We therefore look for ways of letting children make choices about what they want to do and play with. We also encourage children to do as much as they can for themselves so that they can gain in confidence. Alongside this, every child has a key person – someone special who spends time with them and really gets to know them.

Think about it

1 What have you learned about in this unit that links to this pre-school's way of working?

2 Explain how this pre-school is empowering children.

3 Why do you think that this pre-school is known as being a happy place?

Introduction

Babies and children are social beings. From very early on they enjoy communicating and being with others. As part of their development, they learn how to adapt their behaviour so that they can be accepted by others. This is a long process and it is dependent on a range of factors, including their development in different areas, but also the way that adults work with them. In this unit we will look at the factors that affect children's behaviour as well as how early years settings help children show positive behaviour. We will also look at how adults respond to unwanted behaviours.

Assessment: This unit is assessed using a paper-based examination.

Learning aims

In this unit you will:

A understand factors that affect children's behaviour

B understand how adults in early years settings promote children's positive behaviour

C understand how adults support children's behaviour in early years settings.

> I always thought that the way children learn about how to behave was by being told off. Now I know that it is not like that at all. Children learn a lot of their behaviour by watching what adults do. They also need plenty of praise.
>
> Simon, *16-year-old early years student*

Promoting Children's Positive Behaviour

▶ Why children's behaviour may be affected by certain factors

Introduction

There are many factors that affect children's behaviour. Some of these factors are the same for adults.

Discussion point

In pairs, discuss how the following factors might affect your behaviour:

- feeling very tired
- being dehydrated
- having a cold.

Key term

Hierarchy – an order of importance.

Behaviour is not something that is fixed. Like adults, children have moments when they find it hard to control their emotions or to wait to have their needs met. In this section we look at the many factors that can influence children's behaviour, both positively and negatively.

▶ Theories that support our understanding of children's behaviour

There are several theories that adults in early years settings use to understand how to promote children's behaviour. In this section you need to know about Maslow's **hierarchy** of needs and also Bandura's social learning theory. Let's look at each theory before we go on to look at the individual factors that affect children's behaviour.

Maslow's hierarchy of needs

Abraham Maslow devised a theory to explain why humans are motivated to do things. He recognised that people have certain needs that must be met. He also suggested that the needs were ordered and so, for example, the need for shelter, warmth and food had to be met before other needs. His theory of needs is often shown as a pyramid. The needs at the bottom of the pyramid have to be met before those at the top.

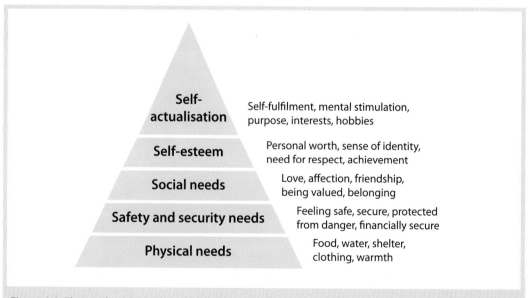

Self-actualisation — Self-fulfilment, mental stimulation, purpose, interests, hobbies

Self-esteem — Personal worth, sense of identity, need for respect, achievement

Social needs — Love, affection, friendship, being valued, belonging

Safety and security needs — Feeling safe, secure, protected from danger, financially secure

Physical needs — Food, water, shelter, clothing, warmth

Figure 4.1 The needs at the bottom of the pyramid have to be met first.

How Maslow's theory is applied to working with children

This theory is used to explain why meeting children's basic needs is so important. The idea is that you cannot expect children to learn and try out new things if they are cold or hungry. In order for children to have **self-esteem**, for example, the needs of the layers beneath must already have been met: they will be well fed and warm, they will have shelter, they will be safe and they will have a loving environment.

Key terms

Self-esteem – how much we value ourselves.

Role models – people from whom children copy skills and attitudes.

Impulsive – when you do something or react to something without thinking about the consequences.

Activity 4.1

Harry is 4 years old. He attends a nursery where he is very happy. Today his mother has let the nursery know that he did not sleep well last night. He also did not want to eat his breakfast. He is now hungry. Harry has just thrown a book across the room. This is not how he normally behaves.

1 What are the factors that are affecting Harry's behaviour?

2 Explain how Harry's needs link to Maslow's theory.

Albert Bandura's social learning theory

Albert Bandura's social learning theory is fairly simple, but very important. The basis behind this theory is that children can learn behaviour and skills by watching others. This learning happens without children being aware of it and so is not the same as an adult telling children to look. Albert Bandura carried out several experiments in which he filmed children. He noticed that children who had seen an adult act violently towards a blow-up doll named 'Bobo' were more likely to repeat the same behaviours when they were put in the same room as the doll.

How Bandura's theory is applied to working with children

If children can learn behaviours and skills by watching, this means that adults have to think about how they are behaving. Adults who shout or are unkind may be teaching children to do the same. The term '**role models**' is often used with this theory. Adult have to be positive role models with children. The idea is that when adults are positive role models, children see how to behave. Of course, children can only copy behaviours that they are capable of, so a baby who is not yet speaking cannot say 'thank you'!

▶ Physical factors

There are a number of important physical factors that can affect children's behaviour.

Sleep

Everyone needs sleep. It is a basic physical need. Sleep plays an amazing role in children's behaviour. This is because sleep is needed by the brain. It helps us to concentrate and manage our emotions, and also keeps us calm and relaxed. There are many effects on children's behaviour if they are not having sufficient sleep for their age and stage of development. One of the most interesting effects is the way that children find it hard to concentrate and also become very **impulsive**. They tend to find it hard to stay still and settle to anything. This makes it hard for them to play, control their behaviour and think through the consequences of their actions.

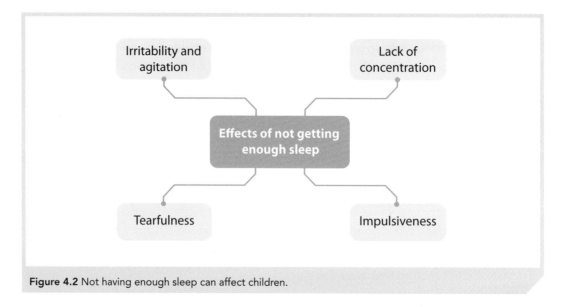

Figure 4.2 Not having enough sleep can affect children.

Discussion point

Sleep is a basic physical need. Using Maslow's theory, discuss in pairs why sleep is needed.

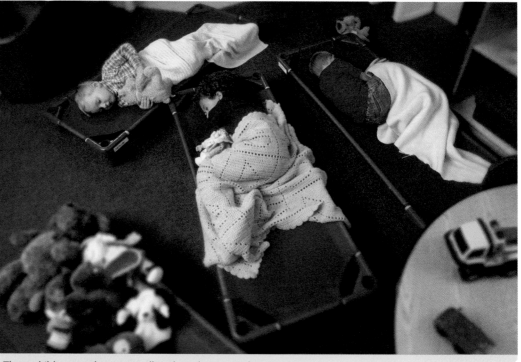

These children need naps as well as their sleep at night.

Food and drink

Key term

Dehydration – where the body does not have sufficient water.

Food and drink is a physical need for children. Young children only have limited capacity in their stomachs. This means that, as well as small meals, they also need snacks. These snacks are part of their diet and so have to be healthy. Children also need sufficient water in their diet. This is why it is always available in early years settings. Lack of water can cause **dehydration** and this in turn affects concentration. This is usually prevented by children having feelings of thirst and asking for a drink. In both adults and children, hunger can also affect concentration. Being hungry and thirsty can make children irritable and they may not cope in situations where they need to be tolerant of others.

Exercise

All children need exercise. For most children, this comes in the form of playing both indoors and particularly outdoors. Exercise helps their concentration and memory, as well as keeping them physically fit. The need to move and exercise is a basic physical need. If this need is not met, children will find it hard to concentrate and enjoy learning. Young children are particularly active and so many play activities allow children to move. Sitting still is hard for children and if they cannot move around, they will often show unwanted behaviour.

Case study

Jamil's family lives in a small flat. The nearest play park is a mile away and his parents do not have a car. He rarely has an opportunity to play outside. His nursery's outdoor area has been flooded for a couple of weeks and so children are not able to use it. Jamil's key person has noticed that during this time Jamil's behaviour has changed.

1   Describe the ways in which Jamil's behaviour might have changed.

2   Explain why the current circumstances may have affected his behaviour.

▶ Biological factors

There are a few factors that can be thought of as biological because they are linked to physical development.

Physical development

Children like to move, touch and hold things. Children may show frustrated behaviours when they have not acquired the skills they need in order to do a particular activity. This might be because of their age or because for some reason their physical development is delayed. They are frustrated because they can see what they would like to do but are unable to join in. Overall we see fewer types of frustrated behaviours with older children because they can do more for themselves without support.

Cognitive delay

The development of children's brains and their cognitive skills is important in behaviour. As children become older and so have more cognitive skills, they are able to remember instructions, think through consequences and change or adapt their behaviours. This means that older children will often remember instructions at the beginning of an activity, but younger ones might forget.

The change in cognitive development as children grow and develop also means that children become less impulsive and are able to concentrate for longer periods. When thinking about children's behaviour, it is important to take age into account. It is also important to think about whether a child has a cognitive delay which may affect their learning. There are many reasons why children's cognitive development may be delayed, including lack of stimulation over a period of time, a brain injury or a learning difficulty. Ways in which their learning might be affected include having difficulty in understanding rules or remembering instructions for how to behave. They may also lack concentration and behave impulsively.

Case study

Lucy is a very typical 2 year old. She often forgets instructions if they are explained to her too far in advance. Her **key person** knows about the cognitive development of 2 year olds. She is patient and knows that Lucy will not always remember instructions.

1 What is the link between Lucy's cognitive development and her age?

2 Why is it important that key persons remember the age of children when thinking about behaviour?

Link

Go to *Unit 1: Patterns of Child Development* where you will find out more information on how communication and language is linked to cognitive development.

Key terms

Key person – an adult who develops a strong, consistent relationship with a child and their family to ensure that a child's emotional needs are met.

Regress – go back to an early stage of development.

Communication and language

Children's communication and language is linked to their behaviour. Once children are talking well, usually by 3 years, it becomes easier for children to manage their behaviour. This is because communication and language allows children to talk about what they want to do and express how they feel. Children who have delayed speech are likely to show more frustrated behaviours, including biting and hitting.

Illness

When children are unwell, they may find it harder to keep to their usual behaviour. Just like adults, they may find it harder to concentrate and become easily upset. They may also be less tolerant. Some medication can affect children's ability to concentrate and it can make children more drowsy. Being unwell also means that children cannot play as easily and so they may become frustrated and even bored. In some cases children may also **regress** and if they have just moved out of nappies, they may need to go back in them. They may also want to be cuddled more than usual and be helped to eat.

How can role modelling lead to positive behaviour?

▶ Social factors

Influences of role models

What children see can affect their behaviour. If children are with adults who are kind and thoughtful, they are more likely to copy these positive role models. On the other hand, if they experience aggressive behaviours, they may start to show these. We also know that children tend to learn from other children too. If they see a child doing something that interests them, they may copy this. This links to the theory that we looked at earlier – Bandura's social learning theory.

Emotional factors

There are some factors that can be thought of as emotional. Children need to feel emotionally safe and secure and to have strong relationships, particularly with parents. This links to Maslow's hierarchy of needs. A sense of emotional security is needed in order for children to go on and learn.

Consistency

Consistency is about knowing what to expect. Children find it hard when adults around them seem to change their moods suddenly and they cannot predict what adults are going to be like. Ideally parents, and especially adults working with children, need to show affection and interest in the child. All children need attention from the people that look after them. If children do not have consistent adults with them, they are more likely to withdraw and not spend time with the adult. Or they may do the opposite and look for ways of getting the adult to react to them, including refusing to do something an adult asks of them. When children do this, it is called **attention-seeking behaviour**. Children who do not feel secure in their relationships are also likely to lack concentration.

Changes in home circumstances

Some types of changes in family circumstances can affect children's behaviours. Small changes such as moving home tend to have short-term effects on behaviour, but significant changes can affect children's emotional security. These might include moving country, the separation of parents or the arrival of a step-parent. Several types of behaviours can result from such changes. These include attention-seeking behaviours, aggression towards adults and other children, but also withdrawal. Changes in home circumstances are hard for children to understand, and they may not have the language to express the emotions that they are feeling. Being unsettled can restrict positive development in other areas. According to Maslow's theory, children will not feel good or confident about themselves unless they feel secure in their home environment.

Cognitive factors

Earlier we saw that cognitive development affects children's behaviour. Here we look at how the cognitive factors linked to the amount of stimulation children receive can play a part.

Stimulation

All children and indeed adults need some stimulation. For children, there is a range of ways in which they may be stimulated. These include playing with toys that are appropriate to their age and stage of development, going on outings and also having time with adults. This attention from adults seems to be very important. When children have sufficient stimulation through the play, activities and learning opportunities on offer in early years settings, they are likely to be more settled and concentrate well.

Link

Go to *Unit 1: Patterns of Child Development* where you will find out more information on the importance of children having a strong bond with their parents.

Key term

Attention-seeking behaviour – behaviours that children show in order to get adults to notice them.

Under-stimulation

Under-stimulation is where there is not enough for children to do or where they are not interested in what is available. A child who has already played for an hour with a train set may no longer find it stimulating. When children are under-stimulated, they become bored and start to look for other ways of gaining stimulation. Unfortunately, these are often not acceptable and in some cases may be dangerous, for example, poking another child with a stick or going down a slide head first. In addition, children who are under-stimulated may use attention-seeking behaviours and try to get reactions from adults.

Over-stimulation

While some level of stimulation is needed, children may find it hard to concentrate when there is too much movement or action or too many things to look at. This is because concentrating means staying focused. If there is too much noise or if there are too many other children running around, children will find it hard to stay calm and play well. Instead, they might become boisterous, over-excited and impulsive. If adults do not take steps to calm children down, this type of behaviour can lead to accidents.

Just checking

1 What is meant by the term 'role model'?
2 Which theory suggests that meeting children's basic physical needs is important so they can show wanted behaviour?
3 What is the link between sleep and children's behaviour?
4 How might communication and language delay affect children's behaviour?
5 Why might feeling unwell affect children's behaviour?

Assessment practice 4.1

Anna is 3 years old. She has just moved flat because her parents have separated. She is not sleeping well in her new room. Her mother said when she brought her into the pre-school that she might be coming down with a cold. During the morning, Anna had a tantrum and later on lashed out at another child.

1 Identify **two** factors that might be affecting Anna's behaviour.
2 Explain how a change in family circumstances can affect children's behaviour.
3 Describe one other factor that can affect children's behaviour.

▶ How settings encourage positive behaviour through provision

Introduction

Early years settings spend time valuing children and helping them to show positive behaviour. They do this in many ways, including by providing stimulation.

The way that early years settings work with children can make a difference to their behaviour. When children are respected and valued, they are more likely to show positive behaviour. In this section we look at ways in which early years settings do this in practice.

▶ Valuing and respecting children as individuals

There are many ways in which early years settings can promote positive behaviours by recognising, valuing and respecting children.

Listening to children

Where early years settings take the time to listen to children and take their views into consideration, this supports children's self-esteem and respect. This is important because if children feel valued, they are more likely to show positive behaviour.

Case study

Apples Day Nursery have been looking at their provision. They have decided to make listening to children a priority.

Explain why this approach might support children's wanted behaviour.

Creating a suitable environment to encourage children to make choices

Empowering children is very important in promoting positive behaviour. Children who feel contented and interested and who have a sense of control over their lives are more likely to show positive behaviour. Where this is not the case, children are more likely to show frustrated behaviours. Early years settings have lots of opportunities for children to make choices and develop their confidence and independence.

Discussion point

Do you remember showing unwanted behaviour as a child when you were bored?

Link

Go to *Unit 3: The Principles of Early Years Practice* where you will find out more information about empowering children.

- **Choosing activities and selecting resources.** Many early years settings will encourage children to choose activities and select resources. This helps children to gain in confidence and feel that they have some control.

- **Choosing where they play – indoors or outdoors.** Many early years settings encourage children to choose whether they wish to go indoors or outdoors to play. This usually happens from 2 years old and is often referred to as 'free flow play'. Children literally move from the indoors to the outdoors and back again without having to ask anyone.

- **Snacks and mealtimes.** Many settings help children to have some responsibility and control by encouraging them to serve themselves at snacks and mealtimes and also offering some choice of foods. With children from around 2 years, settings may also allow children to decide when they wish to have their snack.

- **Responsibility.** Children like having a little responsibility. This is good for their confidence and can also be stimulating and a good learning opportunity. It also means that children feel part of the setting. Early years settings therefore look for ways of giving children responsibility that are appropriate for their age and stage of development.

Link

Go to *Unit 3: The Principles of Early Years Practice* where you will find out more information about helping children's independence by letting them take some responsibility at mealtimes.

Take it further

Visit a local early years setting. Make a list of the ways that children are encouraged to take on some responsibility. Why does this seem to work?

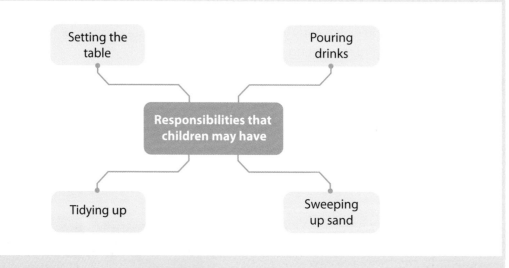

Figure 4.3 Some of the responsibilities that children may have in early years settings.

- **Agreement of expectations.** Children have to know what they can and cannot do. This means that adults have to let children know what is and is not acceptable. These expectations will depend on several things, such as the age of the child and the actual situation. Children find it easier to meet these expectations if they understand the reasons for them and also are involved in setting them. They also need to know what the limits are on their behaviour. These are called boundaries. For example, it might be fine for a 4 year old to be a little cheeky and make everyone laugh, but the boundary is that they should not be unkind or rude. Early years settings will support positive behaviour by talking to children about the expectations and, where appropriate, agreeing them with the children.

Having a key person

Having a key person is important for children's confidence and feelings of security. In terms of promoting positive behaviour, a key person approach works very well – children who have a strong relationship with their key person are more likely to show positive behaviours. This is because they will feel emotionally secure. They will also have plenty of attention and we know that this can prevent attention-seeking behaviours.

Meeting children's physical needs for rest and sleep

Earlier in this unit we saw that children's physical needs play a part in behaviour. Early years settings will try to promote positive behaviour by ensuring that children's physical needs are met, including those for food, drink and exercise. Meeting children's physical needs helps to promote a sense of well-being.

Providing enjoyable, stimulating play opportunities

We know that when children are bored, they may start to show unwanted behaviours. Early years settings try to promote positive behaviour by planning a range of play opportunities and activities that will be challenging for children. This might include cooking activities, painting, outings and junk modelling. It is good practice for these opportunities to be right for children's ages and stages of development, but they should also match the children's interests. In addition, children need opportunities to express their emotions and they gain these from painting and modelling, but also having an opportunity to talk to adults.

Remember

Look back at *Unit 3: The Principles of Early Years Practice*. Describe the role of the key person and why key persons are important for children.

These children are playing well together as they are not bored.

Just checking

1 What do children learn when they are able to select resources in early years settings?
2 Why do early years settings encourage children to be responsible for tasks in the setting?
3 Why do early years settings involve children in the setting of boundaries?
4 Why does a key person approach support children's positive behaviour?
5 Why is it important that children have enjoyable and varied activities?

Assessment practice 4.2

The Darlington Pre-school is looking to promote positive behaviour. They are looking at ways of providing more opportunities for choice for children.

1 Explain why providing opportunities for children to make choices can support positive behaviour.
2 Identify three examples of how a setting might organise their provision and routines to give children choice.

TOPIC   B2

▶ Supporting positive behaviour through boundaries and expectations

Introduction

Like adults, children need to learn that there are certain expectations of how they might behave. They also need to know what they can do. Think about the boundaries and expectations that exist in your school and college. Why are they important?

Most early years settings have behaviour policies. These set out the boundaries and expectations for children while they are at the setting. A boundary sets limits on children's behaviour. For example, it might be fine for a child to shout when outside, but screaming may be discouraged. Expectations are like guidebooks for children. They help to give children ideas of the behaviours they should be showing. It is important that the boundaries and expectations are relevant for children's ages and stages of development.

How early years settings set boundaries and expectations

Boundaries and expectations have to be carefully set, but also communicated to children and any adults who are working in the setting.

Communicating the boundaries and expectations

Having a behaviour policy in a setting is good practice, but also a requirement in many countries' early years frameworks. This document sets out what the setting is trying to promote in terms of positive behaviour and how they intend to do this. Behaviour policies explain how adults must behave in front of children and also how they should deal with any unwanted behaviours. Most behaviour policies will stress the importance of helping children to respect others, stay safe and be thoughtful. The behaviour policy is important as it helps staff to understand what the key expectations and boundaries are in the setting.

This new member of staff is being shown the behaviour policy. Why is this important?

Ensuring that boundaries and expectations are suitable

We know that children's behaviours change with their age and stage of development. The language level of children, for example, will often affect how easy children find it to think through the consequences of their actions. Early years settings therefore have to think about the age group that they work with, and check that expectations and boundaries are developmentally appropriate. In addition, they must think about what would be fair for individual children, given their age and stage of development, and also their personal circumstances.

Where expectations are too low, children miss out on the opportunity to learn some key social skills such as taking turns or thinking about others. On the other hand, where expectations are too high and unrealistic, children are likely not to meet them. This can result in children losing confidence and becoming insecure. They may feel that they can never do anything right. This in turn can make them feel frustrated and, if they are constantly being reprimanded, it can also affect the relationship that they have with the adult.

Remember

Look back at *Unit 1: Patterns of Child Development*. Why are the following expectations inappropriate for a child aged 2 years?

- Sitting down quietly for a long period of time.
- Sharing toys with other children.
- Playing a board game with rules.

Why is it important for adults to base expectations on individual children's ages and stages of development?

Following the behaviour policy of the setting

Children need adults to be consistent. This is why teams working with children need to agree about what the basic principles are in terms of boundaries and expectations. These are normally included in the behaviour policy of the setting. Children are happier when adults seem to give out the same messages. This is especially important with young children who are still learning what the expectations are for their behaviour. There are several consequences if adults do not seem to give out consistent messages:

- **Feeling insecure.** Children like clear boundaries and expectations. Consistent boundaries and expectations help children to feel safe because they know what to expect. If adults are inconsistent, either as a team or as individuals, this can lead some children to feel quite insecure. They may be afraid to try out something new or to join in as they will not be sure whether or not they are doing the right thing.

- **Feeling confused.** Children can also feel confused if adults seem to be constantly changing their mind or when different adults say different things. For example, they may go to one adult who says 'yes' to something, but then another adult tells them that they must stop what they are doing. This can lead to children feeling confused and frustrated.

- **Ignoring rules.** Some children, especially as they become older, either ignore what adults say or work out that they can set one adult against another. They may start to work out which adult is more likely to let them do something and so start to show behaviours that otherwise are not allowed. This 'playing of the system' can mean that children begin to follow only rules that suit them. Although this is quite clever in some ways, it can mean that children start to learn that rules are there to be broken.

Case study

Andie works part-time in a pre-school. She has two grown-up children of her own. As a parent, she proudly says how she did not accept any nonsense and was very strict. In the pre-school she often ignores the behaviour policy and will frequently reprimand children for things that they are allowed to do with other staff members. Today she has stopped a group of children from taking some dressing-up props outdoors. Yesterday another member of staff said that this was fine. The children look disappointed and surprised.

1 Why is it important that staff members agree on boundaries as to what children can and cannot do?

2 Why might the children feel confused about what they can and cannot do?

3 How might being reprimanded for something that you were allowed to do before affect children's confidence?

Ensuring consistency of boundaries and expectations between the home and the setting

As we have seen, children find it hard if what is expected of them keeps changing. Wherever possible, early years settings try to work with parents to make sure that many of the key boundaries and expectations are kept consistent. Being at home and with parents will always be different from being in a group of children at a setting, but there are many expectations which will be the same, such as not hitting others or stopping an action if told to do so. By working with parents, staff at early years settings can help children feel secure and also prevent confusion.

These children know that they must sit down when eating. Is this an expectation that most parents have too?

Helping children understand how to meet expectations for behaviour

As children develop language and more is expected of them, it is important for adults to help children understand the reasons for rules. An adult might, for example, explain that pushing a child down the slide might be frightening for the other child. It is good practice to encourage children to think about what would be fair boundaries and expectations in any given situation. This works well with older children who are at the stage of development when they are interested in rules. If it was raining, an adult might ask the children what they would need to think about if they wanted to play outdoors. This way, the children might be keener to put on their coats or take off muddy shoes when they came indoors.

Reminding children

Young children who are busy having fun often forget boundaries and expectations. Young children do not always apply existing boundaries and expectations to new or different situations, so adults have to remind them. When you remind children is also important. If you remind children too far in advance of the actual time, they are likely to forget. Instead, a gentle prompting to wait for a turn or to ask to get down from the table works better.

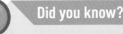
Did you know?

Young children often find it hard to remember instructions. This is because their ability to process words and remember them is still developing.

Encouraging children to value and respect others

Positive behaviour is about being part of a group and respecting and valuing others. Most expectations about children's behaviour is linked to this. Adults help children to learn how to do this by role modelling, but also by reminding children to take turns and being with them to support the sharing of toys and equipment. With babies and toddlers, adults will often 'lead the way' by, for example, saying 'thank you' on their behalf. They may also support toddlers by playing simple games with them that will help them to take turns. Adults will often talk to children about how to play safely and will remind them as well. Children are also encouraged to be polite – this is usually about showing thoughtfulness and respect towards others, for example, letting someone have a turn or saying 'please' in recognition that someone is about to help you.

Encouraging children to take responsibility

As children grow and develop, they need to understand why positive, thoughtful behaviour is important in terms of how it will help them and others. They also need to understand the consequences of their actions and the effects that their actions might have on others. Most children are not developmentally ready to understand this until they are 4 or so. This is because they need sufficient language and cognitive skills. Children often learn to understand the consequences of their actions and the importance of positive behaviour by having their attention drawn to the expressions of others. An adult may spot that a child has offered another child a toy and say, 'Purnima, look how happy you have just made Bethany!'

Just checking

1 What is meant by the term 'boundary' in relation to behaviour?
2 What is the purpose of a behaviour policy?
3 What happens when expectations for children's behaviour are too low?
4 What happens if adults are not consistent in their responses?
5 What might happen if adults have unfair expectations of children's behaviour?

Assessment practice 4.3

Paula is 2 years old. She lives with her foster mother and two other children. She spends five mornings a week with a childminder.

1 Why should staff plan appropriate activities for Paula?
2 Give an example of how her age and stage of development might affect her behaviour.
3 Give two reasons why boundaries and expectations need to be consistent.

▶ Supporting positive behaviour in settings

Introduction

It is recognised that focusing on encouraging positive behaviour is more effective than just looking at unwanted behaviour. Adults can help children show wanted behaviour by talking about positive expectations or acting as good role models.

There are many ways in which we can help children to show positive behaviour. In order to do so effectively, we must always be aware of what can be expected from children in terms of their age and stage of development. It is also useful to remember Maslow's hierarchy of needs and Bandura's social learning theory.

▶ How adults support children's positive behaviour

Modelling desired behaviour

Adults can help children to show wanted behaviour by acting as good role models. There are plenty of ways in which adults can do this, including showing respect for others. For example, helping a child who is struggling to lift a toy not only shows thoughtfulness, but also is an example of good manners. In the same way, role modelling positive behaviour, such as asking for a toy when another child has been using it rather than just taking it, can help children learn good manners and thoughtfulness. Children can sometimes copy the way that adults talk and communicate with others. Adults who do not listen or who often raise their voice are not likely to help children learn how to talk nicely to other people. As you might expect, adults must never use insults or swear words when working with children.

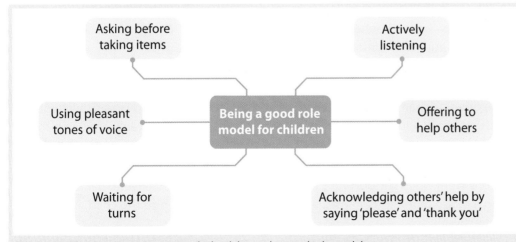

Figure 4.4 There are various ways in which adults can be good role models.

Link

Go to *Unit 1: Patterns of Child Development* where you will find out more information about children's development.

Discussion point

Do you prefer someone to focus on your negative points or your positive ones?

 Did you know

Not all cultures routinely use 'please' and 'thank you' in the same way that we do in English. This might mean that children who are learning English may not know that they should say 'yes, please' or 'no, thank you' when asked a question such as 'Would you like a drink?'

Positive expectations

Adults can help children to show wanted behaviour by having and talking about positive expectations. For example, they may say to children when going outdoors, 'I have put the bikes out because you are so good at sharing.' This is likely to act both as a reminder and as a positive expectation for children. The tone of voice is important in positive expectations, as well as the way in which things are said to children. When adults seem to be negative, it makes it harder to show positive behaviour.

Activity 4.2

Tara is new in an early years setting. She says to one of the children when she lifts the cover off the sand tray, 'I don't want you throwing it around like yesterday.'

1 Why is this not a positive expectation?

2 Suggest how you might let the children know that you are expecting them to keep the sand in the tray in a positive way.

Positive reinforcement

One way of responding positively to wanted behaviour is to use praise and rewards. However, adults must take care to ensure that rewards are meaningful and effective.

- **Skinner's operant conditioning theory.** According to Skinner's operant conditioning theory, we are more likely to repeat a behaviour when there is a **positive reinforcement** or reward which meets a need. All children have a need for attention and so if children are given a smile of approval after doing something, they are likely to repeat the behaviour. Most settings focus on praising children and giving them encouragement in order to help children learn about wanted behaviour. This is because children are more likely to repeat behaviours for which they have been positively acknowledged in some way.

- **Types of rewards.** There are many ways in which settings can provide positive reinforcements which meet children's needs, as Table 4.1 shows.

- **Disadvantages of rewarding children.** There have been some studies that show that always rewarding children for wanted behaviour may mean that children do not carry on if no reward is available. Also in these situations children are not learning the reasons behind why their behaviour is valued by others. Ideally, children need to learn to show wanted behaviour because it makes them feel good inside rather than just to gain adults' attention.

- **Rewards must be meaningful.** Rewards have to be meaningful for the child, otherwise they will not seem like rewards. A toddler is unlikely to understand the value of a star chart, for example, as this is quite a sophisticated reward system. On the other hand, a toddler will enjoy a cuddle and a smile. If rewards are given that are of no interest to the child, they will not be effective.

- **Consistency and continual positive reinforcement.** It is important for adults to be consistent when supporting positive behaviour. Being positive towards children, using a range of reinforcements, including paying attention to the child, is likely to be effective.

Key term

Positive reinforcement – a way of rewarding wanted behaviour so that a child might learn to repeat the wanted behaviour.

Did you know?

Positive reinforcement happens when a need is met. If gaining adult attention is important for children and they get it by shouting or tipping toys into a seated group, this will meet a need and so the children will have had a positive reinforcement. Unfortunately many adults do not realise this and so are surprised when the child repeats the behaviour.

Table 4.1 Types of rewards and positive reinforcements and the reasons why they are positive for children.

Reward/reinforcement	Why it is positive for children
Stickers and stars	• Children like stickers. • Children get attention from adults when they get a sticker. • Children get attention from other children for their sticker.
Verbal praise	• Children are getting eye contact and attention from adults.
Choice of activity or story	• Children get attention from an adult. • Stories are pleasant. • Activity of own choosing is enjoyable.
Points (only for older children)	• Children get attention from an adult when given a point. • Children get attention from other children. • Children know that they will eventually get a further reward.

Discussion point

While positive reinforcement is used in early years settings, there are times when children learn behaviour as a result of negative reinforcement. Negative reinforcement occurs when children do something to change a situation that they do not like, for example, children might come back indoors to put a coat on to stop feeling cold.

There is often confusion over the difference between negative reinforcement and punishment.

- A **punishment** is something that occurs that is unpleasant for the child, for example, the removal of something they are playing with. This is likely to make the child unhappy.
- A **negative reinforcement** is something that leaves the child happier. For example, now that the child has picked up their toys from the floor, the adult has stopped nagging them, or now that they have put their coat on, they are warmer.

Responding to unwanted behaviour using sanctions

One of the ways that settings can encourage children to show wanted behaviour is to let them know that there will be consequences if they continue to show unwanted behaviour. These consequences are often **sanctions**. A sanction could be the removal of a treat or toy. It might also mean the restriction of an activity. For example, a child might be told that they have to stop playing with the sand tray. For sanctions to be effective, it is important to consider the age and stage of the children. Children should be able to understand the sanction and the sanction needs to be relevant and proportional. It is not good practice, for example, to threaten a sanction that will impact on a child's learning and development.

Key term

Sanction – the potential consequence of what will happen if the child continues to show unwanted behaviour.

Key terms

Visual prompts – reminding children by showing them an object or an action.

Visual timetable – a series of pictures that help children to understand what is about to happen.

Responding consistently to prevent confusion

A key way in which adults can promote positive behaviour is by showing consistent approaches. We have already seen this earlier with the idea that children may become confused if adults seem to show different responses. For some unwanted behaviours it is important to keep repeating the same strategy so that the child understands that they will always gain the same response. It is important, though, as we will see later, that the strategy chosen by the adult is the right one!

These containers all have pictures on them. How does this help children to tidy up?

Recognising children's level of understanding and responding

One way in which we can help children is to make it easy for them to understand the expectations that we have of them. As adults, we therefore need to think about their level of understanding and communication. With this in mind, we can then think about how to help them understand our messages. For children with limited language, we might use **visual prompts**, such as pointing to things or, in the case of older children with language delay, using a **visual timetable**. We might also have to remember with younger children that instructions have to be simplified and shorter. Some settings use pictures to help children to remember where things go, which makes it easier for them to tidy away. Staff may also use notices to help remind older children of the setting's expectations of behaviour.

Supervision

Supervision is an excellent way of promoting positive behaviour because it prevents potential unwanted behaviour from occurring. It is a requirement of frameworks that children are properly supervised. In England, for example, it is a legal requirement that children are always either within sight and/or within hearing of an adult. With babies and young children, adults must supervise children constantly, as they have little sense of danger and are quite impulsive. With older children who may sometimes play more independently, adults have to be quick to investigate if there are any of the telltale signs outlined in Figure 4.5.

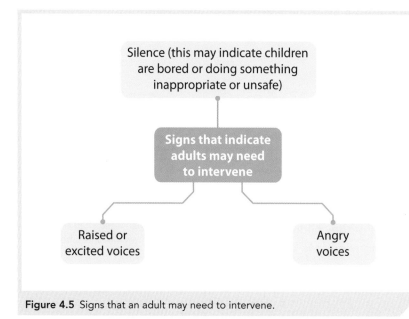

Figure 4.5 Signs that an adult may need to intervene.

Supporting children to solve potential problems

Some adults worry when they hear older children squabbling. Although it is important to keep an eye on this kind of situation, children need to learn the skill of explaining their wishes and ideas to others. If adults feel that children are unable to sort the issue out, it is a good idea to find ways to support children. Adults can sometimes help children to see each other's point of view or can teach children some classic approaches to turn taking and sharing, such as whoever cut the dough or poured the drink does not choose which piece of dough or which cup they can take. The idea when intervening is not to impose a solution on the children, but to help them find ways of resolving their conflict. Sometimes simply asking children whether there are any clever ways that they could resolve their conflict will result in some quite creative and even generous ideas.

Knowing that some behaviours are linked to ages/stages of development

When promoting positive development, adults have to remember that some behaviours are typical for the age/stage of development. Unless adults are proactive in looking for ways to distract children, there is a danger that more unwanted behaviours can happen. Common age-related behaviours for 2 year olds are often linked to frustration, caused by lack of language and also impulsiveness. They include clinging, tantrums, throwing things and snatching. Older children who have some developmental delay may also show these or similar behaviours as well. On the other hand, older children who have good language skills start to answer back.

Just checking

1 Why is it important for adults to model desired behaviour?

2 Which theorist suggested that behaviour can be learned using reinforcements?

3 How do positive reinforcements support children's learning of wanted behaviours?

4 What might be a disadvantage of always rewarding children for wanted behaviour?

5 Why is it important for an adult to investigate if children's voices are becoming raised?

Comparing the effectiveness of methods used to support children's positive behaviour

- **Advantages of using positive reinforcement.** Most early years setting use positive reinforcement as a way of encouraging wanted behaviour. This is because, in the longer term, children are more likely to maintain wanted behaviour. They also start to associate wanted behaviour with positive feedback and adult attention. This helps children develop positive feelings about themselves as being 'good' children and so has a positive impact on a child's self-esteem. There are other benefits too of a positive approach. The atmosphere in the setting feels more harmonious and positive. Children are also more likely to develop better and strong relationships with adults if they are being praised and gaining attention. This in turn will help their learning as we know that when children enjoy being with adults, they are more likely to communicate and listen to them. Role modelling is also important as part of a positive approach. It often means that children firstly see adults showing thoughtful wanted behaviours and this, combined with positive reinforcements, is very powerful. A positive approach also means that children feel respected and, in the long term, this helps children to respect other children too.

- **Appropriate positive reinforcements.** For positive reinforcements to work, it is important that they are relevant to the child and also timely. For example, there is little point in rewarding a child with a party in two weeks' time if they are just 3 years old. In two weeks' time the child is not likely to remember the link between the positive reinforcement and their behaviour. Small positive reinforcements such as praise, a smile or acknowledging that the child has made an effort are always more effective.

- **Disadvantage of using positive reinforcement.** The key disadvantage of using positive reinforcement is that children may start to do things only to please adults and to gain a reward rather than show wanted behaviour for its own sake. It is therefore helpful if positive reinforcements are used from time to time and that adults also encourage children to reflect on how showing wanted behaviour is making them and others around them feel.

- **Advantages of using sanctions.** There are times when sanctions can be very useful, although they are generally seen in early years settings as 'last resort' measures when encouragement and positive reinforcement has not been successful. The removal of the child from an activity or the removal of a piece of equipment that is not being properly used can send out a very strong message and it usually has a strong impact on the child. Sanctions tend to work best for older children who are less impulsive and whose level of cognitive development means that they can understand that their continued action will result in a sanction. Sanctions are therefore usually only appropriate for children over 3 or 4 years of age.

- **Disadvantages of sanctions.** Relying heavily on sanctions is not considered to be good practice. This is because the approach tends to create more stress for both the adult and the child. This can result in negativity. In some cases, children may become angry at having a sanction and this might become a prompt for further unwanted behaviour. Any additional anger or stress in a setting can affect the overall atmosphere in the setting. In addition, if children's behaviour is only managed through sanctions, they may start to develop a **self-concept** of being a 'naughty' child and so over time develop poor self-esteem.

Key term

Self-concept – how we view ourselves.

How adults deal with unwanted behaviour

Introduction

As part of our work with children, we have to know how to manage unwanted behaviour. It is important that it is managed in ways that will not cause other problems for the child. Unwanted behaviour is typical in all ages of children. It is part of growing up.

Strategies for dealing with unwanted behaviour will tie in closely with a child's age and stage. There will also be times when we need to use a different approach, for example, when children have different needs or a developmental delay.

Types of unwanted behaviour

Adults working in early years settings need to be aware of different types of unwanted behaviour:

- attention seeking
- destructive behaviour
- verbal aggression.

Attention seeking

All children need attention. This is because humans are social beings. We all need time when others notice us, talk to us or even just smile. Some children will need more attention than others for a variety of reasons. When children are not getting sufficient adult attention, they are likely to do things that will gain immediate eye contact and attention from adults:

- interrupting activities where an adult may be present
- answering back to prolong the time spent with adults
- challenging instructions to gain eye contact and adult attention.

In addition, some children may show clinging behaviours. This is often a sign that children are needing much more adult time and may be anxious because their parents are not there. Without additional attention, children may become more anxious.

It is important to recognise attention seeking and, as we will see later, make sure that we ignore it while at the same time increasing the overall amount of attention that children have.

> **Discussion point**
>
> With a partner, make a list of things that most children will do from time to time.

> **Discussion point**
>
> In pairs, discuss what it feels like to go somewhere for several hours and for no one to talk to you, make eye contact or acknowledge your presence. Why might children like gaining attention from adults, especially when they are not with their parents?

Why is it important to be patient when children have tantrums?

Destructive behaviour

Destructive behaviour covers a range of different behaviours. There may be various reasons for these.

- **Aggressive behaviours.** These include hitting, biting, kicking, pinching and pushing. For some children, this is linked to their age and stage of development as they may not quite have the skills to be cooperative with others. Sometimes aggressive behaviours in older children are linked to what they have seen or a delay in language.

- **Tantrums and throwing objects.** Tantrums and throwing objects are examples of behaviours often associated with 2 year olds. They are usually 'frustrated' behaviours. Adults have to be patient and calm when children show these behaviours. These behaviours can be seen in other children for a variety of reasons, especially if they are tired or they have delay in their language.

- **Head banging.** Children who bang their head against a wall are likely to be showing us that they are distressed in some way. Rhythmical banging is often a comfort behaviour in the same way that some children suck their thumbs or stroke their heads. If this behaviour is seen, distraction is usually effective and it is important that adults remain calm and gentle. As it is quite unusual, adults may also need to talk to parents about it – it might be a sign that the child is not happy.

Verbal aggression

Some children, once they are talking well, start to use their language in ways that are not appropriate. Name calling and swearing are examples of this. Sometimes these behaviours have been copied from much older children or television programmes. Adults have to intervene when these behaviours are being shown. Intervention has to be sensitive as some children do not know the meaning of what they are saying. They may also not understand how their words affect others either.

▶ Dealing with unwanted behaviour

All children show unwanted behaviour from time to time. Sometimes this behaviour is linked to tiredness, boredom or curiosity. Whatever the behaviour is and the reason behind it, it is essential that adults deal with behaviours sensitively and appropriately.

When to act

The starting point when dealing with unwanted behaviour is to think about whether we need to act and how quickly. There are times when we can wait and just see if children move on and do something else. There are also times when ignoring behaviour is the right course of action, as we will see later. You should always act quickly if:

- there is a danger of a child harming themselves
- there is a danger of a child harming others
- significant damage to equipment or resources is likely.

Thinking about the circumstances

We also need to think about the specific reasons why children might be showing the behaviour. This is important because how we deal with it will depend on why the child is showing the behaviour. Children might be tired, hungry or may have a learning difficulty. Some children may be troubled because their parents have separated.

Discussion point

In pairs, think of five factors that can affect children's behaviour.

Staying calm

One of the most important things that we must do is to stay calm. This helps us to make better decisions and also prevents children from becoming further distressed. A good example of this is if a child has a tantrum. If an adult shows emotion in response to this emotional outburst, the child is likely to sense this. This in turn will lead to more emotion from the child. Being calm also helps children to reduce their anger and frustration levels.

Strategies for dealing with unwanted behaviour

There are a range of strategies that we can use with children if they show or start to show unwanted behaviour. Which strategy to use will depend on the age and stage of the child and their level of understanding. Many strategies do not work unless they are used with children at the right age and developmental stage.

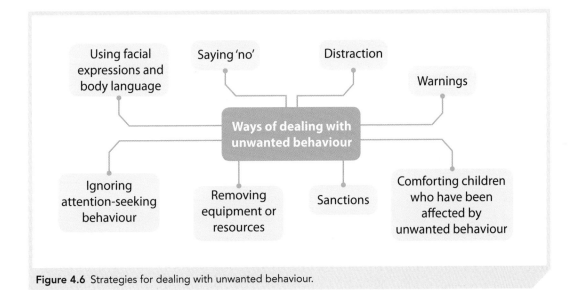

Figure 4.6 Strategies for dealing with unwanted behaviour.

- **Using facial expressions and body language.** Many children will stop what they are doing if the adult is showing disapproval. Adults might frown, cross their arms, point at what the child is doing or stare in the direction of the child. It is important that these signs are a contrast from how the adult usually looks! This means that at other times, we must remember to show signs of approval and that means smiling and looking interested in what children are doing. Facial expressions and body language can work well, as children usually want the approval of adults.

- **Saying 'no'.** Sometimes making eye contact and showing a disapproving face can be combined with a single word, 'no'. This is highly effective if used only occasionally. It does not work if children hear 'no' all the time. It does not work either if it is accompanied by a smile or a giggle, as children tend to notice and work out messages from facial expressions. After saying 'no', adults must make sure that the child does not continue the unwanted behaviour, otherwise 'no' will not be effective the next time.

Figure 4.7 Why is it important for adults not to smile when they say 'no'?

- **Distraction – younger children.** An easy strategy with younger children is simply to give them something else to do or to do something that makes them forget what they were doing. This works well with children under 3 years.

Case study

Sam is 2 years old. He has found a wooden hammer from a peg set and is walking around with it, hitting anything in sight. His key person comes over to him, singing softly and clapping her hands. He puts the hammer down and starts joining in with her. She asks if he would like to look at a book with her.

1 Explain why it was important for the key person to intervene.

2 What is the technique that Sam's key person has used?

3 Why was this a good technique to use with this age of child?

- **Distraction – older children.** Distraction also works well with older children who are showing or in danger of showing unwanted behaviour because they are bored. Playing with them or giving them different resources/toys can prevent unwanted behaviour. This type of distraction usually requires adults to start off the new activity with the children rather than just telling them to go and do something else.

- **Warnings.** With older children, adults can often stop unwanted behaviour by intervening early on and giving children warnings. Verbal warnings work well as adults can explain to children what the problem is and remind them of the boundaries and expectations of their behaviour. Warnings are often given with consequences of what will happen if the children continue with the unwanted behaviour. However, warnings only work if children have enough language and understanding. This means they are usually used with children from 3 years or so.

- **Ignoring attention-seeking behaviour.** Where it is safe to do so, adults should always try to ignore unwanted behaviours that are shown because of attention seeking. This can be difficult to do, but is a very effective strategy. It teaches the child that showing unwanted behaviours does not work. Where an attention-seeking behaviour cannot be ignored because it would be unsafe to do so, a minimum of eye contact and fuss is always best. As attention-seeking behaviour is a sign that a child needs more adult attention, it is important to increase the amount of attention that the child is receiving overall. The trick is to give increased attention when the child is not showing the attention-seeking behaviours.

Activity 4.3

Kamel is 4 years old. He is in the habit of hitting adults on the back to get their attention. Most adults automatically turn around and tell him to stop.

1 Explain what Kamel is learning when adults turn around.

2 Why should adults ignore this behaviour instead?

- **Sanctions.** Children from 3 or 4 years can be told about the consequences if they continue showing behaviour that is not wanted. In simple language, adults explain what will happen if the behaviour is continued. For sanctions to work, they have to be pretty immediate, for example, 'If you keep on throwing sand, the lid will be put on it' or 'If you keep throwing the books, you will not be able to help me mend them.' Sanctions that are longer term, such as 'You will not join in the party this afternoon', rarely work with young children. This is because they might not link the sanction to the unwanted behaviour. If sanctions are threatened, it is essential that adults do carry them out. Otherwise children learn that they can ignore adults!

- **Removing equipment or resources.** Removing equipment or resources can be a helpful solution, particularly when working with younger children. This is because young children can find it hard to 'resist' temptation and so by removing a resource out of sight, a child can change their focus. It is also worth removing equipment or resources that are not appropriate for young children before they even get to see them. This is because young children find it hard to understand why they cannot have something that they see. This strategy can reduce tantrums in toddlers.

- **Comforting children who have been affected by unwanted behaviour.** When there has been an incident that has upset another children, it is important that we take time to support the 'victim'. Sometimes it might mean providing physical reassurance or just explaining the reason why this has happened. A young child might, for example, reach out and knock down a model that an older child has been working on for an hour. Helping this child to understand that the younger child did not do this on purpose, while acknowledging the upset that the action has caused, is helpful. Unfortunately, sometimes 'victims' are ignored and, instead, too much adult time is taken talking to the child who has shown unwanted behaviour. As we have already seen, this is not always a good idea, as sometimes the child who has shown unwanted behaviour learns that they can get adult attention this way.

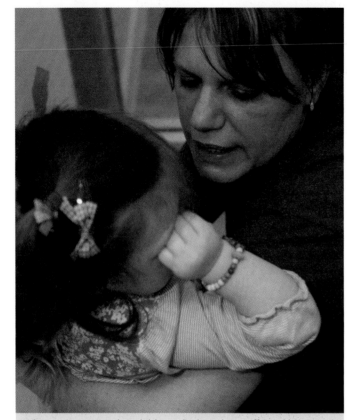

Why is it important that children who have been affected by unwanted behaviour are comforted by adults?

Reporting unwanted behaviour

When children show unwanted behaviour, this often needs to be reported to other adults in the setting. In some cases this will be so that parents can be informed by the child's key person. Who and what to report is normally included in a setting's behaviour policies. It is usual to tell other adults what happened and the circumstances leading up to the behaviour. It is also usual to explain how you managed the unwanted behaviour and how the child reacted. Key persons always need to know what has happened and how it was dealt with, as they know the child best. By having detailed and accurate information, the key person and the parents can together work to support children in showing positive behaviour.

Just checking

1 Why is it important that adults remain calm when dealing with unwanted behaviour?
2 Why is it important to remember the age/stage of the child when dealing with unwanted behaviour?
3 How is distraction used as a strategy for dealing with unwanted behaviour?
4 What strategy works well for attention-seeking behaviour?
5 Why is it important that, if threatened, a sanction should be used?

Assessment practice 4.4

The Happy Days Nursery runs an after-school club for 4 to 8 year olds as well as the nursery. Towards the end of the afternoon the children are mixed in together. As part of the day-to-day work with this age range, staff have to deal with attention-seeking behaviours as well as children who are showing destructive behaviours because they are tired.

1 Prepare an information sheet to help new staff know how they should deal with unwanted behaviour. Your sheet should contain examples of the type of behaviours that are considered unwanted as well as examples of strategies that could be used.

WorkSpace

▶ Maggie Downley

Pre-school owner

We only used to take children who were nearly 3 years or older into our setting. But things have changed in the past year and we now have quite a few young 2 year olds. After so many years of being set up for 3 and 4 year olds, it came as quite a shock, particularly in terms of their behaviour. We soon realised we would have to change the way that we organised our routines and, just as importantly, our expectations. What works for 3 and 4 year olds does not work for younger children. A key turning point was to stop thinking about their behaviour as 'unwanted' but instead to think about it as typical for their age.

We have adapted our ways of working and so we do not have long instructions any more, nor do we make children sit down to an activity. We now expect the odd tussle and, instead of making a song and dance about it, we just try to distract the children. We supervise in different ways too. Adults spend longer playing with children. This seems to help children pick up the skills of turn taking and sharing. Even though we always used to praise children, we now do so in more visual ways such as doing a 'high five' or simply smiling. Long complicated charts have gone. Interestingly, changing our approach has also helped the older children.

Think about it

1 Why did taking in younger children mean that staff had to change their expectations of children's behaviour?

2 What strategies is this setting using to promote positive behaviour?

3 Can you see how strategies to deal with unwanted behaviour are being used in this setting?

Assessment Zone

This section has been written to help you to do your best when you take the assessment test. Read through it carefully and ask your teacher/tutor if there is anything you are still not sure about.

▶ How you will be assessed

The examination will last for one hour and there will be a maximum of 50 marks. The number of marks for each question will be shown in brackets, e.g. [1].

There will be three types of question in the test:

- multiple-choice questions
- short-answer questions worth 1–2 marks
- medium-answer questions worth 4 marks
- longer questions worth up to 8 marks – even if they look hard, you will need to attempt them, especially if you are hoping to do well in the exam.

▶ How to prepare for the examination paper

It is important that you are well prepared before sitting the examination. This means that you will need to revise all areas of this unit. Your teacher/tutor is likely to give you some practice questions and a mock/practice paper to complete. This is a good way to learn examination technique, and how to use your time well.

At the start of the examination, it is a good idea to quickly look through the whole paper. This will calm you down, as you will know what is coming. It will also help you plan how to use the 60 minutes you have to get the best results. Some people rush their answers and sit for 30 minutes doing very little, thinking they have finished, when they could have written better answers. Some people spend too long on the first part of the paper and never reach the end, losing out on many marks.

▶ Hints and tips

- Remember to read the questions carefully, think about them, plan your answers, write your answers and then review what you have written.
- There will be a range of different command words used in the questions, for example 'outline' or 'explain' – make sure you think about these when you are answering each question.
- You should keep moving through the questions and not let yourself get stuck on one. If you are really unsure of an answer or cannot give an answer, then come back to that question at the end.
- Read back over your longer answers. Have you answered the question in full?

Disclaimer: These practice questions and sample answers are not actual exam questions. They are provided as a practice aid only and should not be assumed to reflect either the format or coverage of the real external test.

▶ How to improve your answer

For some of the questions, you will be given some background information on which the questions are based. Look at the sample questions which follow and our tips on how to answer these well.

Sample questions

A Questions where you have to choose from several answers.

Tip: Read the question very carefully. Sometimes more than one answer is required.

Example:

Lack of exercise can affect children's behaviour. Is it **most** likely to make them:

| **A** tired | **B** frustrated | **C** lazy | **D** cheeky |

Answer: B

Setting boundaries and expectations is important in order to promote positive behaviour. Of the following, which two **aren't** necessary?

A being aware of the age and stage of the children

B considering what the children are wearing

C explaining to the children the reasons behind the boundaries and expectations

D making a poster with rules for the children

Answers: B and D

B Questions where you are asked to give a short answer.

Tip: Look carefully at how the question is set out to see how many points need to be included in your answer.

Example:

Define the term 'sanction' and give an example of how it might be used. [2]

Answer: A sanction is the potential consequence of what will happen if the child continues to show unwanted behaviour. Take the child away from the activity if unwanted behaviour carries on.

C Questions where you are asked to give a longer answer – these can be worth up to 8 marks. Sometimes these may be based on a case study.

Tip: Think about how many points you need to make. For a question using the word 'discuss', you must do more than just explain. You might need to talk about the issues or the advantages and disadvantages of an approach. If there is a case study, read the question first and then go back to the case study. Underline anything in the case study that you think is important in order to answer the question.

Harjit is 3 years old. Her parents have just split up and she has not seen her dad for a week. In nursery she has been showing unwanted behaviours such as hitting staff on their back until they turn around and throwing her coat on the floor and then smiling at her key person. When she behaves like this, the staff immediately talk to her and tell her not to continue.

Discuss why Harjit is showing these behaviours and the effectiveness of the setting's approach.

Answer: Harjit is 3 years old and is likely to find the absence of her father difficult. This is likely to be why she is showing a range of attention-seeking behaviours. She needs the attention of staff, but if she is getting this at the time of showing the behaviours, their attention will act as a positive reinforcement. Although it is good practice to talk to children about their behaviour, it would be best if this was not done straight away and if staff ignored the behaviour instead. Staff should also spend more time with Harjit at other times so she learns to gain attention by showing wanted behaviours.

Sample answers and feedback

Read the two student answers below, together with the feedback. Try to use what you learn here when you answer the questions in your test.

Question:

Jasper is 3 years old. He shares a room with his new baby brother, who wakes up several times in the night. At nursery Jasper has become irritable and finds it hard to take turns and share. He sometimes shows aggressive behaviour and hits out at other children from time to time.

1 Describe two factors that might be affecting Jasper's behaviour. [2]

2 Explain two strategies that adults could use to promote positive behaviour. [2]

Student 1's answer

1 Jasper is probably irritable because he does not want to share with his brother.

2 Adults could praise him when he is sharing. They also need to be consistent.

Feedback on Student 1

1 *This student has only provided one explanation for Jasper's behaviour. Key points about the reasons for Jasper's behaviour have been missed.*

2 *The student has given two examples of strategies that the adults could use, but has not given any reasons. The questions asked for an explanation.*

Student 2's answer

1 Jasper is probably tired as his baby brother is waking him up. When children are tired, they are more likely to be irritable. The arrival of the baby brother has changed his home circumstances and he may not be getting as much attention as he did before. He may also be a little jealous of the attention that his baby brother is gaining.

2 His key person could try and spend more time with him so that he feels more secure. It would also be a way of helping Jasper to talk about his feelings. This is important as children's emotional needs have to be met so that they can show positive behaviour. This might reduce his frustration and anger. The setting could also make sure that his physical need for sleep is met by encouraging him to have a nap in the setting. This might help Jasper to feel less irritable.

Feedback on Student 2

1 This student has correctly identified the factors that might be affecting Jasper's behaviour.

2 The suggestions for the strategies were appropriate to Jasper's needs and stage of development. For each suggestion, a clear explanation was given as to why it might support positive behaviour.

▶ Assess yourself

Question 1

Which of these is a cognitive factor that might affect behaviour? [1]

A lack of sleep

C lack of attention

B lack of exercise

D lack of stimulation

Question 2

What do you understand by the term 'positive reinforcement'? [2]

Question 3

What is meant by the term 'role model'? Give the name of the theorist with whom it is associated. Describe two ways in which adults use role modelling to promote children's positive behaviour. [4]

Introduction

Parents who leave their children in early years settings expect them to be safe. They also expect that early years settings will strive to keep their children healthy.

Young children are very vulnerable. They need adults to keep them safe because their understanding of danger is limited. Young children are also prone to infections as their immune system is still developing. In this unit we look at how accidents can occur and ways in which early years settings work to keep children safe. We also look at how infections are spread and go on to learn how early years settings take steps to control the spread of infection.

Assessment: This unit will be assessed through a series of assignments set by your teacher/tutor.

Learning aims

In this unit you will:

A understand accident prevention in early years settings

B understand infection control in early years settings.

> As part of our course, we were shown around a nursery. I was impressed by how clean it was and also by the way that staff checked the outdoor area before letting the children go outside. Now I have finished this unit, I understand why the nursery was so keen on keeping things clean and safe.
>
> Josie, *15-year-old early years student*

Health and Safety in Early Years Settings

5

BTEC

Assessment Zone

This table shows what you must do in order to achieve a **Pass**, **Merit** or **Distinction** grade, and where you can find activities in this book to help you.

Assessment criteria			
Level 1	Level 2 **Pass**	Level 2 **Merit**	Level 2 **Distinction**
Learning aim A: Understand accident prevention in early years settings			
1A.1 Identify why accidents may occur to babies and children in an early years setting.	**2A.P1** English Explain why accidents to babies and children may occur in early years settings, using appropriate examples. **See Assessment activity 5.1, page 149**	**2A.M1** English Discuss how early years settings may reduce the risk of accidents to babies and children, using appropriate examples. **See Assessment activity 5. 1, page 149**	**2A.D1** English Assess the extent to which an early years setting is effective in preventing accidents, using a case study. **See Assessment activity 5.1, page 149**
1A.2 Outline how adults in an early years setting can prevent accidents to babies and children.	**2A.P2** English Describe how adults in early years settings can prevent accidents to babies and children, using appropriate examples. **See Assessment activity 5. 1, page 149**		
Learning aim B: Understand infection control in early years settings			
1B.3 Identify three ways in which babies and children may get infections.	**2B.P3** Describe how babies and children may get infections, using appropriate examples. **See Assessment activity 5.2, page 156**	**2B.M2** Maths Explain the role of the adult in reducing the risk of infections in early years settings, using appropriate examples. **See Assessment activity 5.2, page 156**	**2B.D2** Evaluate the effectiveness of infection control in an early years setting, using a case study. **See Assessment activity 5. 2, page 156**
1B.4 Identify three ways babies and children are at risk from infections in an early years setting.	**2B.P4** Describe why babies and children are at risk from infections in early years settings, using appropriate examples. **See Assessment activity 5.2, page 156**		
1B.5 Outline how adults can reduce the risk of spreading infections to babies and children in an early years setting.	**2B.P5** Describe how adults can reduce the risk of spreading infections to babies and children in early years settings, using appropriate examples. **See Assessment activity 5.2, page 156**		

English Opportunity to practise English skills

Maths Opportunity to practise mathematical skills

How you will be assessed

This unit will be assessed by a series of internally assessed tasks set by your teacher/tutor. Your evidence for this unit will be collected and stored in a portfolio, together with any observation records or witness statements. Throughout this unit you will find assessment practice activities that will help you work towards your assessment. Completing these activities will not mean that you have achieved a particular grade, but you will have carried out useful research or preparation that will be relevant when it comes to your final assignment.

The assignments set by your teacher/tutor will consist of a number of tasks designed to meet the criteria in the table. This is likely to consist of written assignments and may include activities such as producing:

- a guide for parents about how an early years setting prevents accidents to babies and children
- an information file for new staff members about infection control in the setting.

▶ Understand accidents that may occur to babies and young children

Introduction

Babies and young children are more at risk of accidents such as falls, cuts and bruises than any other age group.

Discussion point

Based on your knowledge of child development, can you think of two reasons why children are more at risk of accidents?

In all early years settings, adults spend a lot of their time trying to prevent accidents from occurring. In this section we will look at the reasons why babies and children are more likely than other groups to be at risk from accidents and at the types of accidents that are likely to occur.

▶ Why children are at risk from accidents

There are many reasons why babies and children have a higher accident rate than other groups. The reasons tend to be linked to their development.

Babies and children under 3 years

In this age group there are several features of development that mean they are more likely to have accidents. Firstly, they have no awareness of danger as they are just learning about their environment. They may, for example, not know that wet floors are slippery or that leaning on something with wheels will result in it moving.

Developmentally, children in this age group are also **impulsive**. They see something and focus on getting it rather than on thinking about any dangers.

Key terms

Impulsive – when you do something or react to something without thinking about the consequences.

Mouthing – putting items in the mouth as a way of playing and as a way of exploring them.

Mouthing

Some accidents happen because babies and young children put things in their mouth. This is known as **mouthing** and is a normal stage of development, but if the object is small, it can choke them. In the same way, if the object is sharp, it may cut their mouth.

Children from 3 years

As children grow and develop, they become less impulsive. They can also understand the reasons for things. This means that they start to understand that some things are risky or dangerous. It does not mean that they are safe, because they still forget about dangers. That is why adults have to remind children of this age.

Another feature of this age range is that they have more skills. They are steadier on their feet and can do things they want to more easily.

Children from 5 years

From 5 years old, children are able to understand the importance of safety and of assessing risks, but they still lack experience and are unable to do this consistently. Even in familiar situations they may not be safe, because when play or an activity is very exciting, they may forget what they have been told or what they have promised.

Is there a risk that this baby will choke on the toy?

Why babies and children are at risk from infections in early years settings

There are a number of reasons why children are particularly at risk from infections.

Immature immune systems

Over time, the human body has found many ways of fighting off harmful infections. Special cells and tissues in our body, as well as our organs, are all involved in fighting off 'invaders' by a complex process known as the **immune system**. The immune system in babies and young children is less effective because their bodies are still developing. This means that when children are exposed to a virus or bacteria, they are more likely to become ill than an adult whose body has a greater ability to fight back.

Babies and young children explore objects with their mouth

We have already seen that ingestion often occurs because of babies and young children touching things and then putting objects and hands in their mouth. Unfortunately, it is not possible to stop children from doing this and, as we will see later, it is important for adults instead to try to find ways of minimising risks.

Babies and children are in close contact

Viruses and bacteria love people! The more people there are in close contact, the easier it is for viruses and bacteria to spread. Large settings that may have up to 80 children in them have to work very hard to minimise the risk, especially where children are touching the same objects and breathing air that may contain droplets of viruses and bacteria. It is also interesting to note that more infections occur in the winter months. This is because children in some settings spend longer periods indoors.

Developing bowel and bladder control

Bacteria and viruses can be found in urine but particularly in our **faeces**. As babies and toddlers are in nappies, there is a risk that germs from their nappies can be transferred on to their hands or those of adults during a nappy change.

Even when children are out of nappies, accidents happen. Their clothes or the area where the accident happens can be contaminated with germs.

Key term

Immune system – cells and tissues that work together to fight infection.

Faeces – the solid waste produced by the bowels after food has been digested (poo).

Did you know?

Vaccinations work by exposing children to a virus that has been made safe. Their bodies then produce something called antibodies which will know how to recognise and kill the 'real virus' if ever the child is exposed to it.

If one of these children has a cold, how might it be passed on?

151

Cuts and grazes often occur

Babies and young children often have bumps, cuts and grazes. This is because they are still learning physical skills, such as how to run, jump and walk. Children are also learning about their environment and gaining experience.

This means that they may fall off a tricycle if they go too fast around a bend or slip because they have not realised a surface is wet. As a result, it is normal for children to have a few cuts and grazes.

Just checking

1 Can you identify two ways in which infections can be spread in early years settings?
2 How are viruses like chickenpox spread among children?
3 How might the way babies explore using their mouths increase their risk of infection?
4 What is the link between cuts and grazes and the risk of infection?
5 Why are babies and young children more at risk of infection than older children?

▶ How adults in early years settings can reduce infection risk

Introduction

It is impossible to prevent infection completely, but early years settings have to try to reduce the risk. One of the ways this is done is through hand washing.

Discussion point

Make a list of times when you think it will be important for children to wash their hands. When you have finished this section, see if you missed any!

Key term

Infection control – the ways in which the spread of bacteria and viruses can be minimised.

The term **infection control** is used to talk about the ways in which the spread of bacteria and viruses can be minimised. In early years settings, infection control is taken very seriously and every setting will have policies and procedures which all adults have to follow.

▶ Infection control

There are many ways in which early years settings will put infection control into practice. Many of them are quite simple, but it is essential that adults remember them.

Hand washing

One of the most basic ways that infection can be controlled is through hand washing. Adults touch surfaces, food and of course children, and so can move bacteria and viruses from one place to another or from child to child. By washing hands, adults can remove most of the germs and so prevent the spread. Adults must get into a routine of washing their hands before and after certain activities, as Table 5.2 shows.

Table 5.2 When to wash your hands.

Wash hands before...	Wash hands after...
• changing a child's nappy • touching, serving or eating food.	• a nappy change is over • going to the toilet • going outdoors • blowing nose • using paint, sand, water or other sensory materials.

Supporting children to wash their hands

Adults also have to remind or help children to wash their hands or, in the case of babies, do it for them. The same activities, as shown in Table 5.2, will require children to wash their hands. We may also notice that children have been putting their hands in their mouths and so additional washing may be necessary.

It is important that we help children learn to wash their hands in the most effective way. This requires warm water and soap. Adults also have to make hand washing interesting so that children do not mind doing it. The poster below shows the correct way of washing hands to reduce the amount of germs.

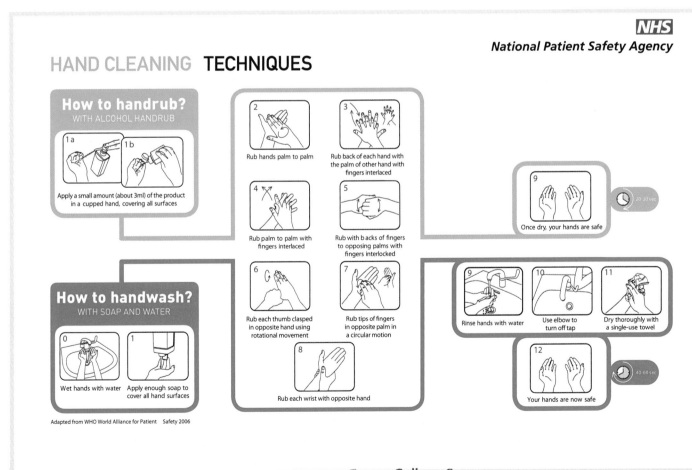

Figure 5.8 Teach children how to wash their hands properly.

Gower College Swansea
Library
Coleg Gŵyr Abertawe
Llyrfgell

Did you know? **?**

Just because your hands look clean doesn't mean that they don't have germs on them. Bacteria and viruses cannot be seen without a microscope.

Reminding children

As well as teaching children how to wash their hands, adults also often need to gently remind children, for example, just before they go to the toilet or come in from the outdoors. It is also helpful to praise children when they wash their hands well or do so without a reminder.

In most early years settings, sinks are at child height to make it easier for them to access the water. Settings also keep an eye out to check that there are plenty of paper towels and soap.

Sneezing or coughing

When we sneeze or cough, we spread millions of droplets containing viruses or bacteria into the air. As we saw earlier, these droplets are breathed in and can make children and adults ill. To help prevent this, the advice is to try to sneeze into a paper tissue or to cover your mouth with a bent arm. Putting a hand across the mouth only works if the hands are immediately washed afterwards.

Settings need to make sure they encourage children to sneeze into a tissue where possible. Paper tissues should always be thrown away after being sneezed or blown into and then hands should be washed.

Acting as a good role model

Key term 🔑

Role models – people from whom children copy skills and attitudes.

One of the ways that we can help children learn to keep healthy is by being good **role models**. Children copy what adults do and so if you wash your hands after you come in from outdoors or put on an apron before cooking, children will learn to do the same. It is important that you act as a consistent role model and follow the routines and procedures of the setting every time.

Wearing disposable gloves and aprons

To prevent infection from spreading on to hands and clothes, it is standard practice for early years settings to use disposable gloves and aprons for carrying out some tasks. These include nappy changing but also clearing up toileting accidents or vomit. This is because bodily fluids such as faeces, vomit, urine and blood can contain germs. Disposable gloves and aprons are then thrown away once the task is finished. To finish off, hands are then washed.

Disposable aprons and gloves are also used when preparing and serving food. This prevents germs from being passed on to the food and so can prevent food poisoning.

Keeping rooms ventilated

We saw earlier that breathing in air that has viruses or bacteria in it can make adults and children ill. A way to prevent the build-up of viruses and bacteria is simply to open a window slightly, especially when it is cold. This is because viruses and bacteria love warm and slightly damp air. By opening a window slightly, air that is not contaminated can come in and the overall amount of viruses and bacteria in the air is reduced.

Washing equipment

At the end of each session in early years settings, toys and equipment are cleaned. This is because children touch them and may put them in their mouths. In settings that have babies, the toys, objects and feeding equipment that babies put in their mouths are also disinfected.

Replacing sensory materials regularly

Sand, water and dough are played with using hands. This means that, after a while, they can contain viruses and bacteria. It is therefore important that these and other sensory materials are regularly replaced. Children should also wash their hands after playing with them. Most settings change the water in water trays so that fresh water is there at the start of each session.

Following routines

Every setting will have routines and procedures that all adults have to follow. Figure 5.9 shows the type of cleaning routines that adults are expected to complete during or after a session.

Washing own clothes

Adults' clothing needs regular washing. Bacteria and viruses can build up on clothing and as children often touch adults' clothing (for example, when hugging), germs can be transferred. This is why many early years settings provide their staff with uniforms that can be washed easily. It is also why for some activities, such as nappy changing, adults have to wear disposable aprons and gloves.

Preparing food safely

Adults in settings have to know how to prepare food safely. Food poisoning can cause children to become very ill and it can sometimes be fatal. Food poisoning is mainly caused by bacteria which can grow very quickly. Most adults in settings are trained to prepare food in ways that will prevent bacteria from building up.

Key points include:

- washing hands before cooking, but also regularly during cooking, especially after raw meat and fish have been touched
- storing food at the correct temperature

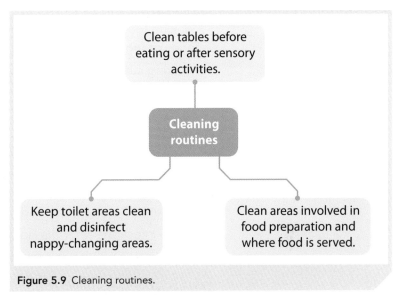

Figure 5.9 Cleaning routines.

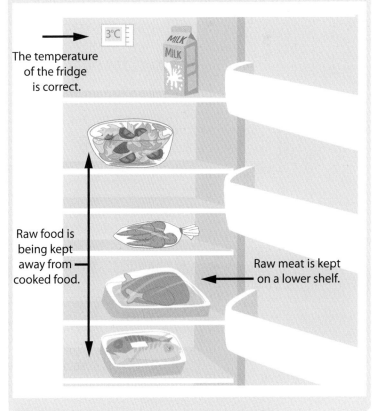

Figure 5.10 Why is it important to store food correctly?

Take it further

When food is kept in a fridge or freezer, bacteria is not killed, but it does grow more slowly. Find out the recommended temperature for a fridge. Go to www.pearsonhotlinks.co.uk, search for this title and click on this activity.

- making sure that fridges or freezers are at the correct temperature (the wrong temperature may allow bacteria to grow)
- keeping raw foods away from cooked ones (raw foods, especially meat, dairy products and fish, can have bacteria on them)
- defrosting food properly. Food that is only defrosted in parts might not be properly cooked later on, and bacteria can grow in those parts
- cooking foods through thoroughly. This is very important when reheating cooked foods or foods that were frozen
- covering cuts with special blue plasters. Cuts can contain bacteria. By covering them, bacteria may not spread. The blue plasters are important because if they fall off, they are easy to spot!

Assessment activity 5.2
2B.P3 | 2B.P4 | 2B.P5 | 2B.M2 | 2B.D2

A group of nurseries and pre-schools have come together to do some training about preventing the spread of infections. You have been asked to provide a handout and some information, using examples, about:

- how infections enter the body
- the ways in which babies and children might be at risk from infections in early years settings
- how adults and early years settings can prevent the spread of infections.

If you have time, one nursery would like you to help them further. They would like you to evaluate their infection control as there have been several outbreaks of food poisoning in their setting. Their manager tells you the following information.

There are procedures in place for hand washing but not all staff follow them. They do provide disposable aprons and gloves for nappy changing, but sometimes they run out. The kitchen is cleaned once a month, including the fridge, but there is not always enough hot water. The staff make sure that children wash their hands before eating, after going outdoors and after going to the toilet. There are also disposable tissues and staff wash their hands after blowing babies' noses.

Tip

- You can use information from a case study provided by your teacher/tutor to support your answer. You will need to make a judgement about how effective the routines, cleaning procedures and ways in which children are supported are at minimising the risks of infection. In your answer you could consider ways in which infection control could be improved.

Just checking

1 Why is it important that children wash their hands after going to the toilet?
2 When should adults wash their hands?
3 How might an adult act as a good role model?
4 What items should be worn when changing a nappy?
5 How can the risk of infection be reduced during food preparation?

WorkSpace

▶ Maria Baker

Childminder

I have been working as a childminder for ten years now. I have ten children who come during the week. The youngest is a 3-month-old baby and the oldest is just 8. Some of the children come every day, but others are part-time. It is quite a challenge working alone and with different ages of children, but I love it. You have to supervise and concentrate on what children are doing all of the time. What is safe for a 5 year old might be dangerous for a baby.

Keeping children safe and preventing the spread of infection is therefore a key part of my work each day and includes:

- thinking about hazards in the home and taking steps to prevent accidents
- using safety equipment
- supervising children and making sure that toys and resources are right for their age and stage
- cleaning toys, resources and all surfaces
- preparing food safely.

When it comes to maintaining hygiene, we do a lot of hand washing! Not only do I have to wash mine to cut down the risk of infections, but I also have to make sure that children do theirs too. Over the years, I have found ways to make this fun and it is now part of the routine.

Think about it

1 Why are the safety needs of a baby different from those of a 5 year old?

2 Why does Maria need to be able to supervise children at all times?

3 Why has Maria picked out hand washing as being particularly important?

Introduction

Learning to talk and understand makes a significant difference to children's development. They can use these skills to express themselves and think. From around 4 years, children begin the journey towards literacy. Being able to read and write helps children to gain more information and also express themselves further. This is important for their later life. Learning to read and write takes time and, before children can start, they need to have developed several skills first. Adults play a major role in helping children gain these skills. In this unit we will look at the role of the adult in promoting children's language and literacy, as well as activities that can work well.

Assessment: This unit will be assessed through a series of assignments set by your teacher/tutor.

Learning aims

In this unit you will:

A understand how to support children's language development

B understand how to support children's reading development

C understand how to support children's writing development.

> I did a placement in a reception class and this unit really helped me understand how to help children with their reading and writing.
>
> Yuksel, *16-year-old early years student*

Supporting Children's Language and Literacy Development

6

BTEC
Assessment Zone

This table shows what you must do in order to achieve a **Pass**, **Merit** or **Distinction** grade, and where you can find activities in this book to help you.

Assessment criteria			
Level 1	Level 2 **Pass**	Level 2 **Merit**	Level 2 **Distinction**
Learning aim A: Understand how to support children's language development			
1A.1 Identify two activities adults use to support children's language development at each age range.	**2A.P1** Explain how adults support children's language development using activities appropriate for each age range, using examples. **See Assessment activity 6.1, page 168**	**2A.M1** Discuss how an adult can be effective in supporting children's language development at each age range, using appropriate examples. **See Assessment activity 6.1, page 168**	**2A.D1** Assess the suitability of support provided by adults for children's language development, for one activity at each age range. **See Assessment activity 6.1, page 168**
Learning aim B: Understand how to support children's reading development			
1B.2 Identify how three activities may support children's reading development.	**2B.P2** Describe how different activities support children's reading development, using appropriate examples. **See Assessment activity 6.2, page 173**	**2B.M2** Explain how adult support may benefit children's reading development, using appropriate examples. **See Assessment activity 6.2, page 173**	**2B.D2** Assess the effectiveness of adult support for children's reading development, using case studies. **See Assessment activity 6.2, page 173**
1B.3 Outline how adults support children's progress in reading.	**2B.P3** Describe how adults can support children's progress in reading. **See Assessment activity 6 .2, page 173**		
Learning aim C: Understand how to support children's writing development			
1C.4 English Identify writing activities for children and the writing development that will be supported.	**2C.P4** English Describe writing activities for children and how writing development will be supported, using appropriate examples. **See Assessment activity 6.3, page 180**	**2C.M3** English Explain how adult support may benefit children's writing, using appropriate examples. **See Assessment activity 6.3, page 180**	**2C.D3** English Assess the effectiveness of adult support for children's writing development, using case studies. **See Assessment activity 6.3, page 180**
1C.5 Outline how adults can support children's writing development.	**2C.P5** Describe how adults can support children's writing development. **See Assessment activity 6.3, page 180**		

English   Opportunity to practise English skills

How you will be assessed

This unit will be assessed by a series of internally assessed tasks set by your teacher/tutor. Your evidence for this unit will be collected and stored in a portfolio, together with any observation records or witness statements. Throughout this unit you will find assessment practice activities that will help you work towards your assessment. Completing these activities will not mean that you have achieved a particular grade, but you will have carried out useful research or preparation that will be relevant when it comes to your final assignment.

The assignments set by your teacher/tutor will consist of a number of tasks designed to meet the criteria in the table. This is likely to consist of written assignments and may include activities such as producing:

- a feature for a magazine to advise adults on how to support children's language
- a leaflet for a library about how adults can support children's reading
- an information file about how to support children's writing.

Adult-led activities to support children's language development

Introduction

Do you remember learning to talk? Most people don't, but we know that all children need to be with adults and to do certain activities in order to gain language. Language is considered to be a route into many other areas of development, including learning to read and write, and for building social skills. Interestingly, when we think, we are actually using language. Sometimes we might even talk aloud when we are thinking!

Discussion point

To see how important language is, make a list of how many times you have spoken to others or listened to others, including the radio, today.

The importance of language

In order to read and write, children need to be fluent speakers of English or the language in which they are learning to read. Language is also needed to help develop other skills. For example, when children are able to understand language and to talk, they can create memories.

Language also helps us to make new connections between what we already know and new experiences and information. Adults play an important role in developing children's language. They help children learn how to communicate, to point out new words and also how to use language to think and to organise their thoughts. In addition, adults can organise activities and new experiences that are right for the children's age and stage and that support the children's language development.

Adult's role in supporting language development

Choosing language activities

There is a range of activities that we can do to support children's language development. Part of the skill in working with children is to match the activity to a child's age, interest and level of development. This is important because otherwise children may become bored and so not participate. If activities are too difficult, there is a danger that children might become frustrated and give up. In order to judge whether an activity might work, the main thing to consider is the child's level of language. Children who are not yet talking well are likely to need activities that are very **visual**.

Speaking clearly

The way we talk can help children to develop language. Children need to hear clear speech as this helps them to learn new words, phrases and also expressions. Speaking clearly includes **sounding out** words and making sure that we are looking directly at children when speaking. Interestingly, our facial expressions and body language can also help children to understand our speech.

Key terms

Visual – this describes something that people look at or watch.

Sounding out – making sure that each sound in a word can be heard by children.

Adapting activities and style of working

While activities can be useful, it is important that we are ready to adapt them to meet children's interests and needs. This might include retelling a story that a child has particularly enjoyed or reading a story on request. It also means that we might need to change our style of working. We might, for example, need to read a story more slowly to help a younger child or allow more time for a child to respond to a question.

Observing children

We also need to check that any activities we are doing with children are enjoyable. This is important because when something is enjoyable, children are more likely to learn. There are many ways of telling whether they are enjoying an activity. We might look to see how interested the children are or how involved they are.

Sometimes if we do not see signs that children are enjoying themselves, we might need to think about adapting the activity. This might mean making a story simpler or putting out story props. It might also mean deciding to end it early. Stopping an activity is always better than continuing something that is not working.

How do facial expressions help children develop language?

Showing enthusiasm and interest

We know that children learn language when adults are enthusiastic and show genuine interest. Children look at our eyes and faces as a way of picking this up. They also look at our body language. When we show genuine enthusiasm and interest, children are more likely to talk and listen. They are also likely to find any activity interesting. This in turn will help them enjoy it, but will also help them learn.

▷ Activities to support language development

There are a number of activities that early years settings use to support children's language development. This is because the language needs of children change as they grow up. This is reflected in the different activities that early years settings provide for different ages and the way that adults carry them out.

▷ Birth up to 2 years

In the first two years of life, children are learning the basic skills of communication, such as making eye contact, turn taking and also understanding body language. They also need to tune into the language they are hearing and to start to use it. They do this at first by cooing and babbling before starting to use first words from around 14 or 15 months. By 2 years, most children are starting to join words together. Adults need to plan activities that will help babies and toddlers to enjoy communicating and also to help them start to understand the meaning of words and to express themselves.

Discussion point

Can you think of an activity that would support a baby's language development? Why wouldn't this activity be suitable for a 4 year old?

Link

Go to *Unit 5: Health and Safety in Early Years Settings* where you will find out more information about safety labels on toys.

Key terms

Vocalisation – making sounds such as babbling and cooing as well as early talk.

Treasure basket play – discovery play for babies where all the objects are made from natural materials.

Encouraging vocalisation and turn taking

Some activities and ways of working with babies and toddlers are about encouraging **vocalisation**. This might be cooing, babbling or, for toddlers, attempts at their first words. Babies and toddlers also have to learn that communication is a two-way process, with each person taking their turn. Activities that can work well include adults playing with finger puppets or making a soft toy, such as a teddy bear, come to life. Babies and toddlers often laugh and smile when they see this, especially when adults put on funny voices. It is important, though, that a gentle approach is used so as not to scare babies and toddlers.

If you use finger puppets and soft toys, make sure that they are clean and safe. Some soft toys can cause babies and toddlers to choke.

Encouraging children to talk and be interested in what they are experiencing

Children are more likely to talk if they are doing or seeing something that they find interesting. Early years settings will therefore plan activities that will be exciting or different for babies and toddlers. There are many things that can be planned and for babies these might include **treasure basket play**, water play and also offering finger foods. Outings such as going to see the trains or going to a park or play area where there are swings are also used. These activities only work if adults talk to the children and take an interest in what children are looking at or wanting to talk about.

Supporting listening skills

Some activities are planned that will help children listen and hear new words. This will help babies and toddlers because before they can say a new word, they first of all have to recognise and know it. There are many activities that can help, including the use of rhymes.

Rhymes, especially finger rhymes, seem to help babies and toddlers because they enjoy the sounds and the repetition of words. These rhymes also help children feel included and learn the importance of turn taking that is involved in communication. Favourite rhymes include 'This Little Piggy Went to Market' and 'Tommy Thumb'.

How can treasure baskets support development?

Some settings use rhymes as part of their routines and so a finger rhyme such as 'This Little Piggy Went to Market' might be sung or said at nappy changing time. This helps babies and toddlers to learn rhymes more quickly. By working in this way, we enable babies and toddlers to know what to expect and often they will take their turn in communicating. They may, for example, make eye contact with the adult at key points during the rhyme.

Encouraging repetition

We have seen that finger rhymes are often used as part of a routine to help babies become familiar with the sounds and words in rhymes. Some action songs have plenty of repetition within them and so they are often used to help children learn new words. Popular action songs include 'Row, Row, Row the Boat' and 'The Wheels on the Bus'. Adults will often help babies to enjoy these rhymes by putting the babies on their laps. Toddlers usually sit or stand to copy the adults.

Activity 6.1

Find the words to 'The Wheels on the Bus'. See how many times words are repeated in this song.

▶ 2 years up to 5 years

There is a huge change in children's language development in these three years. Children move from using simple words to being able to talk in full sentences. The role of the adult is crucial in this period. Children need plenty of time with adults and lots of opportunities to talk and learn new words.

Encouraging children to speak

Many children in this age group love seeing puppets. We can use hand puppets and finger puppets with them. While hand puppets are often best used by adults (since we can make them come to life), children often enjoy holding and using finger puppets themselves. Many children love animals, so it is worth looking out for some animal hand puppets and especially ones that have moving mouths. This seems to help children want to talk back to them. Some hand and finger puppets can be used during storytelling.

Why might you use hand puppets to tell a story?

Key terms

Expressive language – speech that allows children to express themselves.

Vocabulary – all the words a person knows.

Encouraging expressive language

As children develop language, we need to encourage them to talk and to express themselves as much as possible. This is called **expressive language**. We also need to widen their **vocabulary**, which is about increasing the number of words that they know and use. There are many ways of doing this, as we will see, but a key way is through the type of materials and experiences that are planned. We know that children often pick up new words and talk more when they are actually doing something and so interesting activities, such as cooking and gardening, can work well. For example, when children are cooking, they may hear and use new words such as 'grater' or 'stir'.

Encouraging development of vocabulary

Action songs are one of the ways in which we can encourage children to learn new vocabulary and words and then to use them. Children are quick to learn and join in with action songs such as 'Hokey Cokey'. It is worth knowing, though, that many children join in with songs but don't always know what the words mean.

It is a good idea to talk to children about the meaning of words, although the advantage of some action rhymes is that children can work out the meanings because of the actions. Popular action songs include 'The Farmer's in His Den' and 'Ring a Ring o' Roses'. Another benefit of action songs is that children enjoy feeling part of a group.

Action songs can help children to develop their vocabulary.

Supporting the development of listening skills, new vocabulary and expressions

Through listening activities, children can pick up a range of new words and expressions. The best listening activities also involve children talking. This gives them the chance to repeat and use what they have heard soon afterwards. This means that activities that allow children to join in are particularly good.

Look out for stories that you can tell that have repetitive lines such as 'Goldilocks and the Three Bears' or 'The Three Billy Goats Gruff'. Children also enjoy listening activities such as picture lotto and 'guess the sounds'. Both of these games you can make yourself.

▶ 5 years up to 8 years

Between the ages of 5 and 8 years, most children are now fluent in speech. They are starting to enjoy talking and using their language to play games, think and even to argue! There are many activities that adults can use with children to encourage the development of thinking skills and to develop their language further.

Encouraging children to use language to express themselves

With increased language, children can enjoy opportunities to express themselves in a variety of different ways. They love making up songs and jokes but also enjoy making up plays and acting things out. This can include creating mini plays for puppet shows. Some children can also go on to writing scripts for their plays and puppet shows. Children love to have an audience for their work and so adults should take an active interest and provide positive feedback.

How could acting out a play help children to develop their language?

Encouraging the development of language to express thoughts

Activities that encourage children to think about what they are doing can help children to use their language to organise their thoughts. For example, when making a model, a child might talk about what they hope to construct and also talk through any difficulties that they are having. There are plenty of activities that can help children to express their thoughts. These include modelling with clay or other materials and looking at objects, such as buttons, that require sorting in some way.

Take it further

Using the internet or resource books, see if you can find three games that would be suitable for children aged 5–8 years that will promote their listening skills.

In order to develop children's language to express their thoughts, adults have to work alongside children and have conversations about what they are doing.

Encouraging listening with games

Older children enjoy social games that have rules. Games such as 'Simon Says' or 'sound lotto' are great fun and help children to develop listening skills. These types of games can also help children build their vocabulary.

Encouraging the development of new vocabulary

One of the ways in which we can help children learn new vocabulary is to take them on outings where they see new things and have different experiences. This means that many early years settings organise outings, but also encourage parents to take children to varied places such as a local museum, farm or a historical place such as a castle or house. Simply going to a new place is not enough in itself, as adults need to talk to children about what they are seeing. They also need to give children opportunities to point out things of interest or to talk about what they are noticing.

Just checking

1 Why is it important to choose language activities that are appropriate to the age/stage of the child?

2 How does speaking clearly to children help their language?

3 Why are new activities and experiences used to help children's language development?

4 Why is it important for adults working with babies to use action songs and rhymes?

5 What sort of skills might a group of 6-year-old children learn from social games with rules, such as 'Simon Says'?

Assessment activity 6.1 | 2A.P1 | 2A. M1 | 2A.D1

You have applied to be an assistant to a childminder. As part of the interview process, you have been asked to plan two activities detailing how to support children's language. As this childminder works with children from 0 to 8 years, you need to do the following, providing examples.

• Explain how the types of activities you have planned can be used to support children's language development at different ages.

• Discuss how adults might use the activities to support children's language development at different ages.

• Assess the effectiveness and suitability of adult support for children's language development when using the activities at different ages.

Tip

• You have to write about how adults support language for each age group of children. There are three age ranges: 0–2 years, 2–5 years and 5–8 years.

▶ Activities to support children's reading development

Introduction

To help children learn to read, we need to allow them to share books with adults and introduce them to the shapes and sounds of letters.

In order to read, children need a wide range of skills. They need to understand that spoken words become print and that sounds that we say become letters. There are many activities that early years settings will plan to help children do this.

Sharing books with children

Children can learn a lot about reading from sharing books with us. Children can see that, in English, print travels from left to right. It is also read from top to bottom. Most early years settings plan times when children can share books with adults. The best way of sharing books is to make sure that children can properly see the pictures and the words, so sitting with a child next to you works well. Sharing a book with an adult also helps children to love books and be interested in learning to read. Books can be used with babies as well as toddlers and older children. It is important that the right type of book is used with children. This means thinking about the age/stage of development. For babies, we might use fabric and simple board books which mainly have pictures. With toddlers, books that have good pictures and repeated phrases work well. Older children who can concentrate for longer enjoy books that have **plots**.

Encouraging recognition of familiar words

It is helpful if children start to recognise a few familiar words. This encourages them to notice letters and also to see the link between letters and sounds. The first word that children start to recognise is their name. Early years settings plan activities to help this. They may, for example, ask children to find their name at the start of the session or at snack time. Treasure hunts are a good way of helping children to enjoy finding their name and other words. Early years settings might also put up captions on pictures and point them out to children.

Discussion point

Write down the letters of the alphabet in both capital and lower case letters. How many different letter shapes do children need to recognise?

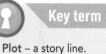

Key term

Plot – a story line.

What are these children learning about stories and books?

169

Making books with children

Helping children to enjoy books can help them become interested in reading. As an activity, many early years settings make books for and also with children. The children might draw pictures or take photographs which are arranged and put into a book. Adults then write captions based on what children want to say. This helps children to link specific words with print. They also learn about page layout and that print is read from left to right in English.

Activity 6.2

Make a list of five activities that could be photographed and turned into books. An example has been done for you.

1 *Making a cake.*

Singing nursery rhymes for younger children

Children have to learn that sounds that we say link to individual or groups of letters. Before this can take place, children need to be able to hear individual sounds in words e.g. the 'ck' in 'lick'. It is known that nursery rhymes can help children do this as they help children focus on the rhythm and individual sounds. Children may, for example, listen out for the 'ck' sound in the nursery rhyme 'Hickory Dickory Dock'. Nursery rhymes can be sung or said. The more rhymes that children know, the easier they find it to read.

Activity 6.3

Make a list of ten different nursery rhymes, including 'Five little peas in a pea pod pressed'.

1 Write out the words and also say them.
2 Which sounds do you find yourself focusing on and saying a little bit more loudly?

Saying rhymes, phrases and tongue-twisters

Rhymes, phrases and **tongue-twisters** are fun and work well with children from around 3 years or so. They particularly enjoy rhymes, phrases and tongue-twisters that have words beginning with the same letter, for example, 'She sells sea shells on the seashore.' This is known as an **alliteration**. Rhymes and phrases with alliteration help focus children on the initial sounds in words. When children first start to read, these phrases and rhymes can help children to link a letter with a sound.

Playing sound games

Another way of hearing sounds in words is by playing games. These can be played once children are talking well. Therefore, they are often played just before children begin school. Games are a great way to help children learn sounds. They are fun and so children learn effortlessly. Common games include sound lotto or 'I spy'. Some musical games are also used to help children learn to listen to general sounds.

Key terms

Tongue-twister – a sentence that is fun but tricky to say because words begin with similar sounds, e.g. 'She sells seashells.'

Alliteration – where two or more words in a sentence or phrase begin with the same letter.

Playing word games

Once children are starting to read, some activities can be planned to help children practise their learning. Early years settings might organise treasure hunts with messages for children to follow or they might plan word games including Junior Scrabble®.

? Did you know?

While there are 26 letters in the alphabet, these combine to make 44 different sounds in English, for example, 'ee' 'sh' 'tion'

Just checking ✓

1 Why is it important that books are shared with children that are appropriate to their age/stage of development?
2 What do children need to learn about page layout when reading English?
3 Can you think of two ways of helping children learn familiar words?
4 What is meant by the term 'alliteration'?
5 How do sound games support children's reading?

TOPIC **B2**

▶ Adult's role in supporting children's reading skills

Introduction

Adults play an important part in helping children to enjoy reading. This is important because children who enjoy books are more likely to spend time looking at books.

In this section we look at ways in which adults can support children to enjoy reading and so develop their skills.

Choosing books and activities

A major role of adults is to make sure that books and activities are right for children's age and stage of development, and particularly their language development. Children need the first books and activities that they experience to be enjoyable. This then helps them to be interested in reading.

- **Choosing books for younger children.** Toddlers enjoy reading books that have good pictures and simple stories, but also have a physical element. They like flap books, for example, or books that make a noise when a button is pressed. Young children also enjoy books that have different **textures** for them to touch or that have holes in them. With an adult, children also enjoy looking at books where there are characters hidden in the illustrations for them to find.

💬 Discussion point

In pairs, consider whether or not you enjoyed reading as a child.

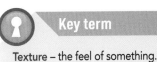

🔑 Key term

Texture – the feel of something.

171

Key term

Fiction – books that have a story.

Non-fiction – books that have information on the real world.

Take it further

Visit a bookshop or library and find an example of each of the following:

- a cloth book for a baby
- a 'touch and feel' book for a 1–3 year old
- a storybook for a 3–5 year old
- a non-fiction book for a 5–7 year old.

Choosing fiction and non-fiction books

Adults have to choose books that are right for children's language development, but also their interests. There are two types of books that children might like. There are **fiction** books, which have a story, and **non-fiction** books, which are about the real world – for example, space or animals. Children might enjoy both type of books, but it is important to choose books that they will like. As well as books, children might also like looking at other reading materials. These could include comics and text on computers or other screen devices.

Reading books clearly with expression and enthusiasm

The way we share books with children can make a difference. Children need adults to look interested in books and to read them with expression and enthusiasm. For example, if you are reading a story that has characters, you might create 'voices' for each character. When reading a non-fiction book, you might talk about how interesting a fact is and encourage the child to look closely at a detail. It is also important to read clearly as children need to hear the sounds in words as part of their learning. If you do not know a book well or if you find it hard to read aloud, it can be a good idea to practise first.

Responding to children's interests when sharing stories

Being read to or sharing a story with an adult should be fun for children. Children who have enjoyable experiences are more likely to want to pick up a book and look at it by themselves. They are also likely to start to look at words on a page. We can make reading a book fun by involving children. For example, we can encourage them to turn the pages or talk about what is happening. We should also make sure we reply to children's questions as well as talk to them about what they are reading or hearing.

Giving children time to look at books

When we are sharing books with children, we need to go at their pace. Some children like spending quite a lot of time looking at pictures, but others like to know what happens next. When children are first learning to read, it will take them quite a while to work out what each word says. Hurrying children can make them lose confidence and so it is important to not to rush them. Sometimes when children are first reading, they like to reread a sentence or page that they have just read. This helps them to remember the words more easily.

How can you encourage children to engage with the story when reading to them?

Knowing which rhymes are appropriate for the age of the child

All children enjoy rhymes. At first, these might be nursery rhymes and songs, but as children's language develop, they often like rhymes that are more challenging. Look out for poems and also simple **riddles** and **limericks**.

Key terms

Riddle – a puzzle in the form of a question that requires some thought in order to answer it.

Limerick – a type of poem that is rhyming and usually humorous.

Just checking

1 Why is it important to choose books and activities that are appropriate for the age/stage of children?

2 When reading aloud, why is it important for adults to speak clearly?

3 What is meant by the term 'fiction'?

4 When sharing a story, why is it important to respond to children's interests?

5 Why is it important to give children time to look at books?

Take it further

Using the library, internet or other resources, find the following:

- two nursery rhymes for 0–2 year olds
- two poems for 2–4 year olds
- two riddles for 4–7 year olds.

Assessment activity 6.2

2B.P2 | 2B.P3 | 2B.M2 | 2B.D2

You have been asked to plan activities that will help support children's reading development in settings 1 and 2. In your plan you must:

- describe the different activities that can be used to support children's reading in both settings
- give examples of how certain activities can benefit children's reading
- explain and assess the role of the adult in supporting children's progress in reading.

To help you provide examples and also to illustrate the importance of the adult role, information about two settings have been provided. You can use this information to assess the effectiveness of the adult support on offer.

Setting 1

In this setting, adults spend a lot of time sharing books with children. They take great care to choose books that they feel will be right for the children's stage of development and their interests. The adults also make sure that reading books is an enjoyable activity. They encourage children to take their time and to feel involved in the reading process. The setting does not plan rhymes or sound games.

Setting 2

In this setting, adults do not actively encourage children to read or share books. They believe that if the books are available, the children can go and look at them. On the other hand, they do plan rhymes, songs and sound games. These are enjoyed by the children. Adults also take care that the rhymes and games work well for the children's age and stage of development.

Tip

- Provide examples to clarify how adults support children's reading. You should also consider the strengths and weaknesses using the case studies provided by your teacher/tutor.

▶ Activities to support children's writing development

Introduction

Can you remember learning to write? For most children, writing begins by making marks on paper. This might be moving a crayon over a piece of paper or painting. In this section we look at the type of activities that early years settings use to encourage children's early writing skills. These activities often develop children's hand movements.

Discussion point

In pairs, make a list of the physical movements that you need to do in order to copy out this sentence using a pen and paper.

Key terms

Gross motor movements – large movements of the arms and legs.

Fine motor movements – small movements usually associated with the hands.

Palmar grasp – wrapping the whole hand around an object to make a movement.

Tripod grasp – a pencil hold where the finger and thumb hold the pencil, supported by the middle finger.

Pincer grasp – using finger and thumb to hold a small item as if pinching.

Link

Go to *Unit 1: Patterns of Child Development* where you will find out more information about gross motor movements and fine motor movements.

▶ Skills for writing

It is worth understanding the skills that children need in order to write. Reading and writing are linked and so children need to be able to recognise the shapes of letters and also how the letters link to sounds. But, as children begin writing using a pencil and paper, there are physical skills that children also need to develop. Let's have a look at these skills.

Gross motor movements

First of all, children need good control of their arm movements. This means that early writing activities for children under 4 are often based on large movements, or **gross motor movements**, of the arms. Children may, for example, be given a large roll of paper on to which they can make marks.

Fine motor movements

A range of small movements made by the hand are important for writing. These are also called **fine motor movements**. Children need to have strength in their hands and fingers. They also need to be able to hold and control a pencil. At first, children will hold a pencil using a **palmar grasp**, but from 3 years, they will be encouraged to use a **tripod grasp**. This grasp helps with later joined handwriting. Developing the tripod grasp begins with a **pincer grasp**.

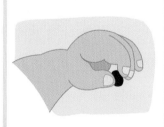

Figure 6.1 The pincer grasp helps children to develop a tripod grasp.

Figure 6.2 At first, children will hold a pencil using the palmar grasp.

Figure 6.3 The tripod grasp is important for later handwriting.

Motivation

As well as gaining physical skills, children also need to have a positive attitude towards writing. This means that activities have to be enjoyable.

▶ Activities that support writing development

Painting

Most early years settings provide opportunities for children to paint from around 18 months. Painting usually comes before drawing as children can use whole arm movements. Painting opportunities are provided by putting large sheets of paper on easels or on to tables or walls. Children can then stand to paint using large and small brushes. At first, children enjoy the sensation of painting, but at around 3 years, children start to create pictures.

Activities like painting help to support children's development.

Drawing

Children often enjoy drawing from the age of 3 years. They enjoy using a range of resources, including markers, felt tips, crayons and pens. Drawing requires fine motor skills and so it helps children's **fine manipulative movements**. It also gives children confidence and a chance to express themselves.

Mark-making activities

The first type of writing activity that early years settings provide for young children is known as **mark making**. When children are mark making, they are making lines, circles and other marks. From this, they may go on to experiment with making letter shapes. All these activities are important as they are the first step towards writing. Most mark-making activities use **sensory** materials. Children might, for example, make lines or marks in damp sand using their finger or a stick. Other materials include cornflour and water, known as gloop and foam soap. Mark-making activities not only help children's fine motor skills but also help them to understand the link between expressing your ideas and making marks.

Scribing

Children also enjoy it when adults write things for them. They might ask an adult to write a caption on a drawing or help them to write a message. This is called **scribing**. It helps children to see the link between spoken words and written words. By watching adults, children also learn how to form letters and learn that writing in English goes from left to right.

Key terms

Fine manipulative movements – intricate movements of the hands, showing concentration and skill.

Mark making – a stage of learning to write in which children are encouraged to make marks, using a wide range of resources.

Sensory – sensory materials are resources that feel interesting and which children can explore, such as sand and dough.

Scribing – writing exactly the words that a child wants to be recorded.

Annotating

As part of learning to write, children also enjoy **annotating** or labelling. They may pretend to write a shopping list or write on to a blank sticker. They may also try to sign cards or, after drawing a picture, write a line about it. At first, this writing is made up of circles and lines, but quickly children start to pick up some letter shapes. By the time children have finished their first year in school, they are likely to be writing simple sentences.

Writing opportunities

Many early years settings create areas where children can write. They may put out a range of pens, crayons, markers to go with pads, diaries and notepads so children can have a go at mark making and writing. As large-scale opportunities are important, most settings also provide whiteboards and markers and also chalkboards. Most settings also provide opportunities so children can 'pretend' as they are writing. Resources include shopping lists and other props, which are often put in role-play areas.

> **Key term**
>
> Annotating – writing a caption so that others can understand mark making or early writing.

My clowns are funny
Charlie is squirting water

Figure 6.4 This child has written about his picture.

Just checking

1 Why are fine motor movements important for writing?
2 What type of tools could be used to develop children's handwriting skills?
3 Why is it important for children to have enjoyable early writing experiences?
4 What type of materials can be used to support children's early writing?
5 How can providing shopping lists encourage children's writing development?

▶ Adult's role in supporting children's writing development

Introduction

Learning to write requires many skills and takes children quite a time. Adults can help children gain the knowledge and skills that they require.

The role of the adult is quite varied when it comes to supporting children's writing. Adults have to provide activities for children, but also need to make sure that children are motivated to write. There are many ways in which adults can do this.

Recognising children's age/stage of development

Children's mark making and early writing goes through certain stages which are linked to their development and to the opportunities that they have had.

- At first, children spend time making marks. Lines and circles are very common with 2 and 3 year olds.
- The next stage is for children to start making shapes that look like letters. Quite often these are linked to the letters in their name, as this is something that they have often seen adults write. It is also one of the first words that children recognise. We see lots of 3 and 4 year olds doing this. By the time children start school, many are just about forming their names.
- The next step usually comes when children are at school and starting to read. They start to be able to write a few more words.
- By the age of 5 or 6, children can write simple sentences.

> **Discussion point**
>
> Why do you think that it is important that adults recognise the stage of development of each child?

Figure 6.5 At what age do you think a child would draw this?

Recognising how children are doing in their writing is important for adults. It means that we can make sure that we put out resources that they will find interesting and enjoyable, but also safe.

Joining in with early writing activities

A great way of encouraging children to write and to practise their mark-making skills is to plan activities together. We might, for example, put out a large sheet of paper and sit with children and also do some writing. This helps children because they can see that writing is something that is fun and also they can watch us to see how to hold a pencil or make a certain shape. Other activities where we might join include putting out brushes and water outdoors and making movements on the ground or putting a shopping list in the home corner and joining in with their play. When we join in with children in this way, we act as positive **role models**.

Checking that materials for early writing are attractive

Children are more likely to mark when everything they use works and looks nice. A felt tip that is dried out is not likely to interest a child for very long. An important role of the adult is to make sure that what is put out is suitable. This means that pencils and crayons need to be sharpened, felt tips and markers are checked and there is sufficient paper. In most early years settings there are also areas for mark making and early writing. These areas have to be attractive so that they look interesting for children.

Key term

Role models – people from whom children copy skills and attitudes.

Link

Go to *Unit 2: Promoting Children's Development Through Play* where you will find out more information about adult-led and adult-initiated play.

Case study

Arnie is a student on placement in an early years setting. His supervisor has asked him to set out the writing table this morning. There are plenty of resources available, including different colours and sizes of paper, notepads, envelopes and a range of markers, crayons and felt tips. Arnie is not interested and so puts out just a few crayons and a few plain pieces of paper. He does not sharpen the crayons or put out any other resources. During the session the supervisor notices that the children are not using the writing table. She starts to add in more resources. She gets out a red cardboard box and makes it into a postbox. Very shortly afterwards, the children start to come and have a go at writing. They try writing letters and post them in the newly made postbox.

1 Explain why at first the children did not go to the writing table.

2 Explain why children were interested in writing letters afterwards.

3 What other materials and resources could also have been put out to support this play?

Forming letters

Children can learn a lot about writing by watching adults and noticing what they do. A child might see how to form the letter 'D' after watching an adult write 'David' on a picture. There are many opportunities for children to watch adults write. Adults might write captions on children's work or children may ask adults to write down their words for them. It is therefore important that adults form their letters in ways that are correct for the style of handwriting that children are learning. This can vary from setting to setting.

There are different styles of handwriting, including printing, when letters do not join, and cursive, where letters are joined. Some schools start by showing children how to print, but others start with cursive writing. The starting points for forming letters are different according to the style. One of the first words that many children write is their name.

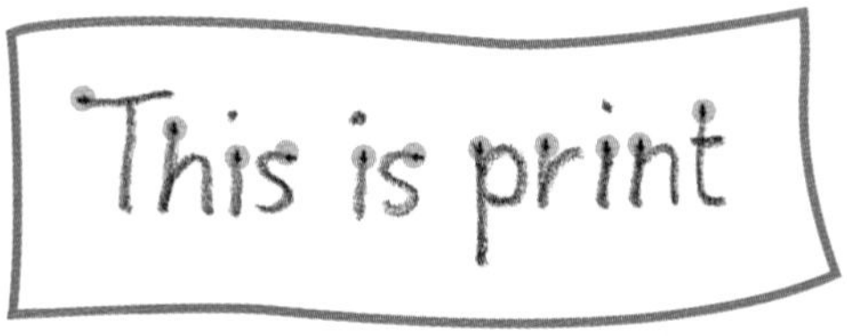

Figure 6.6 An example of print handwriting.

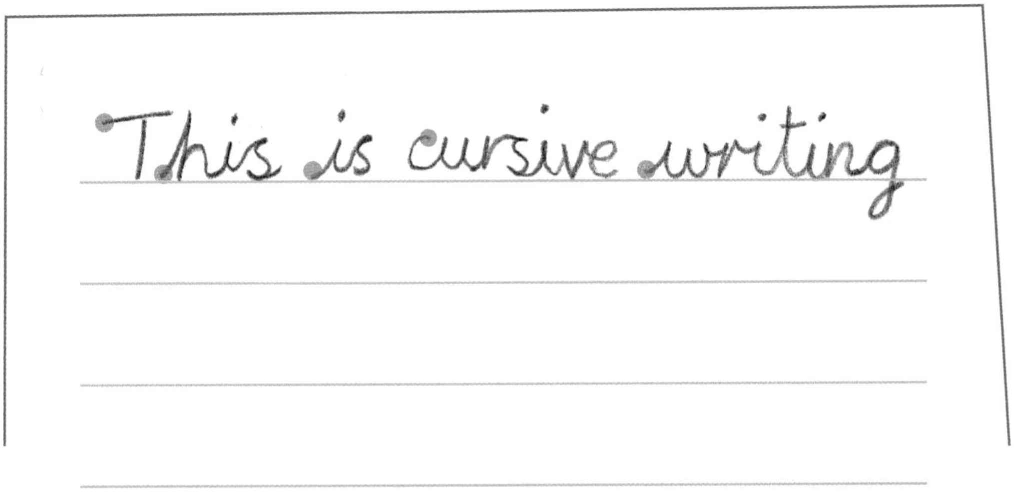

Figure 6.7 The starting points for cursive handwriting are different.

Take it further

Do some research online to find activity sheets that help children practise letter formation for the whole alphabet, both for print and cursive writing.

Positive feedback

Children need a lot of positive feedback when they first begin mark making or start writing letters and words. They need to understand that it is fine not to be able to write everything down correctly. This is important because when children are concerned that they have to get everything right, they are more likely to write less. The role of the adult therefore is to provide this positive feedback. This means acknowledging what children have done and taking an interest in it. We might say things such as 'That looks interesting. Did you enjoy doing this?' Sometimes we might ask a child whether they would like to know how to write a letter or word as well. This approach is better than correcting them. Instead of feeling that they have done something wrong, they are making a decision to learn something new.

Just checking

1 Why is it important to plan writing activities that are appropriate for children's age/stage?

2 What are the benefits for children when adults join in with writing activities?

3 Why do adults need to ensure that writing materials are attractive?

4 Why is it important for adults to role-model correct letter formation?

5 Why is it important to give children positive feedback when they write?

Assessment activity 6.3

2C.P4 | 2C.P5 | 2C.M3 | 2C.D3

The Foundation unit takes children between the ages of 3 and 5 years. It is based in a primary school. The school is keen for the children to make good progress in their early writing. There are opportunities for children to write indoors and outdoors. There are chalkboards, large white boards and always a writing table on offer. The staff take great care to make sure that the pens, markers and other items on the table are interesting. They often create a mini office, complete with staplers, Post-It notes and envelopes to motivate children. For the younger children, the setting also puts out sensory materials such as damp sand, brushes and water. The adults in the setting sometimes join in with the children and talk to them about their marks and writing.

The Foundation unit has asked you to explain their work to new parents. You should prepare a presentation that looks at:

- the type of writing activities that support children's development
- the role of the adult in supporting children's writing development, using examples
- how adult support can benefit children's writing development, using examples.

The Foundation unit has also asked you to provide an assessment of their support for developing children's writing.

Tip

- Foundation units are created when schools mix their reception classes with their nursery classes.
- You need to give examples of how adults might support children's writing. You should also consider both the strengths and weaknesses, using the case studies provided by your teacher/tutor.

WorkSpace

▶ Jan King

Childminder

I have worked with children since I left college. At first, I worked in a nursery, but after having my own children I decided to become a childminder. I love working in my own home. I have eight children on my books aged from 6 months through until 7 years. They are here for different amounts of time. Some of the older ones come every day after school, while one of the babies is with me only for three mornings a week. As a childminder, I am responsible for not only their health and safety, but also their development, including language and literacy. I plan many activities including:

- sharing books
- singing rhymes and songs
- going on outings
- putting out mark-making and early writing materials
- playing sound games, including 'I spy' with the older ones.

It is not just about planning activities, though. You have to work in ways that mean that children want to chat and communicate. You also have to adapt the way you do things according to the age of children. Babies need a lot of attention and plenty of smiles and eye contact. Older children enjoy chatting and you have to be a good listener. You also have to be positive when they first learn to read and write.

Think about it

1 Why does Jan use rhymes and songs to support children's communication and language development?

2 Why is it important that Jan works in different ways according to the age of children?

3 Why is going on outings an important activity for all age groups?

Introduction

What children eat and drink can make a difference to their health and well-being. Food and drink is needed for energy and growth. Children need energy to play and to learn new skills. This is why adults working with children need to provide children with healthy food and drink. This is actually more complicated than you might think, as children's food and drink needs change according to their age and activity levels.

Healthy food and drink is also very important for helping children to stay well and to have good concentration. Adults can help children make healthy food choices and try to create mealtimes and snack times that are enjoyable. They also need to know about food labels and what is in food and drink products. This is because some children may become ill if they have a certain type of food. In this unit we look at the types of food and drink children need at different ages and also at the ways in which adults can help children to eat a healthy, balanced diet.

Assessment: This unit will be assessed through a series of assignments set by your teacher/tutor.

Learning aims

In this unit you will:

A understand the importance of a balanced diet to meet the nutritional needs of children from birth up to eight years

B understand how adults can support children's dietary needs.

> Before I did this unit, I did not know anything about creating healthy meals and snacks for children. I have learned so much. It's even made me think more about what I eat!
>
> Hayley, *15-year-old early years student*

Making Healthy Food Choices for Children

7

This table shows what you must do in order to achieve a Pass, Merit or Distinction grade, and where you can find activities in this book to help you.

Assessment criteria			
Level 1	**Level 2 Pass**	**Level 2 Merit**	**Level 2 Distinction**
Learning aim A: Understand the importance of a balanced diet to meet the nutritional needs of children from birth up to 8 years			
1A.1 Outline the components of a balanced diet and their food sources.	**2A.P1** Describe the functions of each component of a balanced diet. **See Assessment activity 7.1, page 197**	**2A.M1** Assess the specific dietary requirements of children to support their growth and development as they progress from birth up to eight years. **See Assessment activity 7.1, page 197**	**2A.D1** Analyse a child's selected meal and snack plan for a day, ensuring all components of a balanced diet are met. **See Assessment activity 7.1, page 197**
1A.2 Identify the benefits of a balanced diet on children's health.	**2A.P2** Explain the importance of children's diet on their health and development, using appropriate examples. **See Assessment activity 7.1, page 197**		
Learning aim B: Understand how adults can support children's dietary needs			
1B.3 Identify reasons why some children may require a specific diet.	**2B.P3** Explain different reasons why a child may require a specific diet. **See Assessment activity 7.2, page 206**	**2B.M2 Maths** Assess how adults in a selected early years setting support children's individual needs and encourage healthier food choices, using a case study. **See Assessment activity 7.2, page 206**	**2B.D2** Analyse the effectiveness of adults in supporting children's dietary needs, using a case study. **See Assessment activity 7.2, page 206**
1B.4 Identify ways in which adults encourage children to make healthier food choices.	**2B.P4 Maths** Describe ways in which adults in an early years setting can encourage children to make healthier food choices. **See Assessment activity 7.2, page 206**		

 Maths   Opportunity to practise mathematical skills

WorkSpace

▶ Helena Downing

Nanny

I look after two children, aged 2 and 5 years. I have been doing this for six months. This is my second nannying job. It's hard work, because you are responsible for all aspects of children's care and education. At the same time, it is great to be so involved with the children.

As part of my responsibilities, I have to prepare food and serve it. This is easy to say but I have to think about:

- making sure that the food I buy and prepare is in line with the parents' wishes
- buying food to a budget
- making sure that the food that is served is healthy and balanced
- encouraging the children to try out new tastes and textures
- sitting with the children at mealtimes
- involving children in the preparation and serving of the food.

When I first started as a nanny, I was a little worried about this aspect of my work, but I found that there were plenty of online resources. My cooking skills have also improved!

Think about it

1 Why is it important that Helena encourages the children to try new tastes?

2 Why is it important for Helena to listen to the parents' wishes?

3 Why is it good for Helena to sit with the children at mealtimes?

Introduction

Working with children requires a set of skills and attributes that are essential. This means that you need to have certain characteristics if you are interested in working in the early years sector. Some of these skills may seem quite basic, such as being reliable and punctual, but are needed whatever the job role. Other attributes include being patient and enthusiastic, and having a sense of humour. These skills and attributes are looked for by employers and parents when they are choosing adults to work with children. There are many different job roles within the early years sector. If you are interested in working with children, it is useful to know what types of jobs are available in order to plan a career. For some job roles, you will need to have specific qualifications, knowledge and experience. In this unit we look at the skills and attributes that you need to work with children. We also explore the types of settings, roles and responsibilities which adults wanting to work with children might choose.

Assessment: This unit will be assessed through a series of assignments set by your teacher/tutor.

Learning aims

In this unit you will:

A investigate the role of workers in different types of early years settings

B explore roles, responsibilities and careers in the early years sector.

> Before I did this unit, I did not know that there were so many different jobs working with children. I now have an idea of what I want to do and also what qualifications I will need to have.
>
> Amrita, *16-year-old early years student*

Introduction to Working in the Early Years Sector

BTEC Assessment Zone

This table shows what you must do in order to achieve a **Pass**, **Merit** or **Distinction** grade, and where you can find activities in this book to help you.

Assessment criteria			
Level 1	**Level 2 Pass**	**Level 2 Merit**	**Level 2 Distinction**
Learning aim A: Investigate the role of workers in different types of early years settings			
1A.1 English Identify the personal attributes and qualities for work in the early years sector.	**2A.P1** English Explain the personal attributes and qualities required for work in the early years sector, using appropriate examples. **See Assessment activity 8.1, page 221**	**2A.M1** English Discuss how the personal attributes and qualities of workers in an early years setting support children's wellbeing, learning and development, using a case study. **See Assessment activity 8.1, page 221**	**2A.D1** English Assess the contribution of the personal qualities and attributes of early years workers in an early years setting to a child and their family, using a case study. **See Assessment activity 8.1, page 221**
1A.2 Identify early years settings suitable for families with differing childcare needs.	**2A.P2** Select, with reasons, early years settings suitable for families with differing childcare needs. **See Assessment activity 8.1, page 221**		
Learning aim B: Explore roles, responsibilities and careers in the early years sector			
1B.3 Identify the roles, responsibilities, qualifications and experience required for one job role in childcare and education, and a job role in management in the early years sector.	**2B.P3** English Describe the roles, responsibilities, qualifications and experience required for a job role in childcare and education, and a job role in management in the early years sector. **See Assessment activity 8.2, page 228**	**2B.M2** Compare the roles, responsibilities, qualifications and experience required for a job in childcare and education, and a job in management in the early years sector. **See Assessment activity 8.2, page 228**	**2B.D2** Evaluate how a combination of qualifications and experience may enable progression to different roles in the early years sector. **See Assessment activity 8.2, page 228**

English Opportunity to practise English skills

How you will be assessed

This unit will be assessed by a series of internally assessed tasks set by your teacher/tutor. Your evidence for this unit will be collected and stored in a portfolio, together with any observation records or witness statements. Throughout this unit you will find assessment practice activities that will help you work towards your assessment. Completing these activities will not mean that you have achieved a particular grade, but you will have carried out useful research or preparation that will be relevant when it comes to your final assignment.

The assignments set by your teacher/tutor will consist of a number of tasks designed to meet the criteria in the table. This is likely to consist of written assignments and may include activities such as producing handouts, leaflets and articles for a careers event that help others find out about working in the early years sector.

▶ The personal attributes and qualities required for work in the early years sector

Introduction

There are many qualities that you need if you are to work with young children. This is because adults working with children are very influential.

Key term

Attribute – a quality or feature of a person.

Discussion point

In pairs, make a list of five things that you think are the most important when it comes to choosing someone to work with children. When you have finished this topic, see if you have changed your mind.

Regardless of what job role you take, there are some attributes and qualities that you will need to have. These are often looked at in interview situations. Each **attribute** and quality is in important in its own right, but together they are likely to support children's well-being and development. As most of our work with children involves working closely with children's families, some qualities and attributes help parents to trust us. This is important, as leaving a child with someone whom you do not personally know can be difficult for parents. Let's look at the many attributes and qualities that organisations and employers look for.

Genuine interest in children and their development

Anyone working with children effectively has to be genuinely interested in children and child development. It is not enough just to like playing or being with children. This is because to work professionally with children requires us to understand what children are doing and why. Adults who are interested in children and child development are more likely to know how best to support children's development. This can have the following results:

- Adults may plan activities that will promote children's skills and identify where children need additional support. This in turn means that children are more likely to be more successful at school than they otherwise would have been.

- Children who have been supported in this way may also be happier and have learned social skills that allow them to make friends.

- An interest in child development and in the individual children that you work with will also mean that children who may have particular needs or additional needs are more likely to feel supported and so reach their potential.

Link

Go to *Unit 1: Patterns of Child Development* where you will find out more about child development.

A practitioner has chosen this activity because she knows about child development and this child's needs.

▶ Unit 4

Assess yourself

Question 1: Which of these is a cognitive factor that might affect behaviour? [1]

A lack of sleep   C lack of attention

B lack of exercise   D lack of stimulation

Answer: D

Question 2: What do you understand by the term 'positive reinforcement'? [2]

Answer: A positive reinforcement is way of rewarding wanted behaviour so that a child might learn to repeat the wanted behaviour.

Question 3: What is meant by the term 'role model'? Give the name of the theorist with whom it is associated. Describe two ways in which adults use role modelling to promote children's positive behaviour. [4]

Answer: A role model is someone who shows wanted behaviour. Children learn by watching them to copy the wanted behaviour [1]. The term 'role model' is associated with the theorist Albert Bandura [1]. An adult might say 'thank you' when receiving something. Children hearing this might start to use it too [1]. An adult might hold up the door to let another adult go first. Children might see this and copy this thoughtful action [1].

A

Additives – chemicals that are added into foods to provide flavour or colour, or to give them a longer life.

Adult-initiated play – play opportunities set up by adults for children to discover.

Adult-led play – play opportunities and activities that are organised and led by an adult.

After-school provision – a place where children can go at the end of the school day.

Alliteration – where two or more words in a sentence or phrase begin with the same letter.

Annotating – writing a caption so that others can understand mark making or early writing.

Asthma – a long-term lung disease in which the airways become inflamed and narrow.

Attention-seeking behaviour – behaviours that children show in order to get adults to notice them.

Attribute – a quality or feature of a person.

Autoimmune disease – a disease where the body attacks itself.

B

Bacteria – cells that multiply quickly to infect the body.

Balanced diet – a diet providing sufficient nutrients for the age of the child.

Beriberi – an uncommon disease caused by a significant lack of vitamin B1.

Bookkeeping – recording financial transactions.

Breakfast club – a place where children can go before school starts and where they may have breakfast.

Budget – the total amount of money available for an organisation to spend.

Burns – burns are caused by something hot but dry touching the skin.

C

Carbohydrate – a type of nutrient found in foods such as bread, rice, potatoes and pasta.

Cell – a tiny part of the body.

Centile chart – a chart on which measurements are marked and compared with those of other children of the same age.

Chicken pox – a viral infection, common in childhood, that causes spots and a slight fever.

Child-initiated play – play in which children choose what and how to play, and who to play with.

Choking – difficulty in breathing caused by a blockage in the windpipe.

Coeliac disease – an autoimmune disease that results in a person not being able to digest gluten.

Components – several parts that, when put together, create something else, e.g. a balanced diet.

Conserve – an understanding that a fixed quantity of objects or liquid remains the same, even if it is presented differently.

Cooperative play – taking part in play with other children.

CSSIW – a Welsh organisation responsible for inspecting early years settings.

D

Daily nanny – a nanny who comes to the family's house each day.

Defect – something that is not properly formed.

Deficiency – when something is lacking.

Dehydration – where the body does not have sufficient water.

Developmental norms – the milestones that are associated with a particular age group.

Diabetes – a disease that results in the body not processing or making enough of an essential hormone called insulin.

Dietary exclusions – food that for a variety of reasons is not eaten.

Dietician – a health professional who provides advice and guidance about eating.

Digestion – a process by which food is broken down and can be used by the body.

E

Eczema – a skin condition that causes skin to become red and itchy.

Emotional security – a feeling of being cared about.

Empathy – the ability to imagine what someone else is feeling.

Empowerment – giving children involvement in decisions that affect them, appropriate to their age and level of understanding.

Expressive language – speech that allows children to express themselves.

F

Faeces – the solid waste produced by the bowels after food has been digested (poo).

Fat – a type of nutrient that provides energy.

Fatal – a fatal accident or incident is one that causes a death.

Fibre – a substance found in fruit and vegetables that aids digestion.

Fiction – books that have a story.

Fine manipulative movements – intricate movements of the hands, showing concentration and skill.

Fine motor movements – small movements usually associated with the hands.

Fortified – when additional vitamins and minerals are added into food at the time of manufacture.

G

Gluten – a substance found in wheat, barley and rye.

Gross motor movements – large movements of the arms and legs.

Growth – the division of cells.

H

Halal – this describes food that is prepared in accordance with the requirements of Islam.

Hand–eye coordination – where eyes and hands work together to manage a task.

Hand preference – the hand that is most often used for tasks requiring hand–eye coordination and which will become the hand used for writing.

Head circumference – the measurement of the head from above the eyebrows to around the back of the head.

Health visitors – health professionals who advise families with children.

Heuristic play – play in which children learn from discovering a range of objects.

Hierarchy – an order of importance.

HMRC – Her Majesty's Revenue and Customs, the agency that deals with tax and national insurance.

Holiday club – a place where children can go during the school holidays.

Holistic development – the development of a child, taking into account all aspects of what they can do, not just one single area of development.

Hormones – chemicals that can trigger cell division, creating subsequent growth.

I

Immune system – cells and tissues that work together to fight infection.

Impartial – when someone is impartial, they do not take sides and are not easily influenced.

Impulsive – doing or reacting to something without thinking about the consequences.

Incident – an event that might affect children's safety or well-being.

Inclusive practice – ways of working that make children feel welcomed and ensure that their needs are met.

Index finger – the finger next to the thumb.

Indiscriminate attachments – where babies show affection and can be cuddled by people they do not know.

Infection control – the ways in which the spread of bacteria and viruses can be minimised.

Ingestion – swallowing.

Inhalation – breathing in.

Initiative – recognising that something needs to be done and doing it.

Inspected – checked by the relevant inspectorate.

Inspectorate – an organisation that checks settings are complying with legal requirements.

Insulin – a hormone that is essential to the health of the body. It helps to regulate the amount of sugar in the blood.

Intolerances – where food causes a mild reaction.

K

Key person (key worker) – an adult who develops a strong, consistent relationship with a child and their family to ensure that a child's emotional needs are met.

Kim's game – a game where several objects are shown to children before one is taken away. Children have to use their memory to work out which object is missing.

Kosher – this describes food that is prepared in accordance with the requirements of Judaism.

L

Lactose – a type of sugar found in milk and dairy products.

Lactose-intolerant – a difficulty in digesting lactose that results in an allergic reaction.

Limerick – a type of poem that is rhyming and usually humorous.

Live-in nanny – a nanny who lives in the family's home.

Locomotive movements – skills involved in crawling, walking, running and being mobile.

Loose part play – play in which children can explore objects that have been deliberately left outdoors for them to find.

M

Malnutrition – where a diet lacks nutrients or does not have them in the right quantities.

Mark making – a stage of learning to write in which children are encouraged to make marks, using a wide range of resources.

Micronutrient – a nutrient required in tiny quantities, but which is essential for health.

Milestones – skills or pieces of knowledge that a child has acquired.

Minerals – types of nutrients that the body needs in small quantities for good health.

Mouthing – putting items in the mouth as a way of playing and as a way of exploring them.

Mucous membranes – the linings of body cavities that are exposed to the air; for example, the nose, mouth and ears.

Muscular dystrophy – a disease that causes the muscles to become gradually weaker over time.

N

Negatives – a way in speaking and in writing of saying that something is not the case or is not present. This is achieved in several ways, including words such as 'not', 'no one' and 'nothing'.

Non-fiction – books that have information on the real world.

Norovirus – a strain of virus, sometimes known as the 'winter vomiting bug', which causes severe sickness and diarrhoea.

Nurtured – feeling valued, protected and supported because someone is taking care of you.

Nutrients – substances found in food that are essential for health and growth.

Nutritious – food and drinks that support a healthy diet.

O

Obese – very overweight.

Ofsted – the English organisation responsible for inspecting early years settings and schools.

P

Palmar grasp – wrapping the whole hand around an object to make a movement.

Perception – the ability to become aware of something by using the senses.

Personal pronouns – words such as 'it', 'she', 'he' and 'they' which replace someone's name.

Pincer grasp – using finger and thumb to hold a small item as if pinching.

Plot – a story line.

Plurals – a way in speaking and in writing of communicating that there is more than one object or person. This is usually achieved by adding an 's' to a word, e.g. 'dogs'.

Policy – statement explaining the principles that the setting is using to keep children healthy and safe.

Positive reinforcement – a way of rewarding wanted behaviour so that a child might learn to repeat the wanted behaviour.

Pretend play – also known as imaginative play. Children pretend that they are other people or pretend that toys are real.

Primary carers – people who have a significant role in a child's life – often, but not always, the child's parents.

Procedure – a breakdown of the steps involved in implementing different parts of a policy.

Protein – a type of nutrient found in foods such as meat, fish, eggs and milk.

Proximity – the nearness or close physical distance between the adult and the child.

Puncture wound – a wound caused by something sharp entering into the skin, e.g. a splinter.

R

Reflexes – instinctive movements in babies, including startle, sucking, rooting and grasping.

Regress – go back to an early stage of development.

Rickets – a disease that causes bones to soften and break.

Riddle – a puzzle in the form of a question that requires some thought in order to answer it.

Role models – people from whom children copy skills and attitudes.

Rooting – instinctive movement that helps babies to find the breast or the bottle's teat.

S

Sanction – the potential consequence of what will happen if the child continues to show unwanted behaviour.

Scalds – scalds are caused by something hot but wet touching the skin. This includes steam.

Scribing – writing exactly the words that a child wants to be recorded.

Scurvy – an uncommon disease caused by a significant lack of vitamin C.

Self-concept – how we view ourselves.

Self-conscious – being aware of oneself and of what others might think about you.

Self-efficacy – a belief in one's own potential abilities.

Self-esteem – how much we value ourselves.

Self-image – the way that you view yourself.

Self-serve – being able to choose items without asking permission.

Sensory – sensory materials are resources that feel interesting and which children can explore, such as sand and dough.

Sensory impairment – a difficulty with one or more of your senses, for example, your sight, hearing or touch.

Separation anxiety – panic and distress shown when a child cannot see or be with their parents or people they are emotionally close to.

Settling in – the process by which children become familiar with the setting and their key person.

Small-world play – play with miniature characters, animals or other objects.

Sounding out – making sure that each sound in a word can be heard by children.

Specific attachments – where babies and young children show affection and can be cuddled or reassured only by their primary carers.

Staff appraisals – when a manager considers the work of individual staff members so as to develop their practice.

Starchy foods – a food group that is high in the nutrient carbohydrate.

Startle reflex – instinctive movement when babies fling out their arms in response to sudden sounds or movements.

Suffocation – difficulty in breathing caused by the mouth and nose being covered.

Symptoms – signs associated with an illness.

T

Texture – the feel of something.

Tongue-twister – a sentence that is fun but tricky to say because words begin with similar sounds, e.g. 'She sells seashells.'

Transitions – long- or short-term changes that affect the child's life, for example, starting pre-school or changing carer.

Treasure basket play – discovery play for babies where all the objects are made from natural materials.

Trial and error learning – learning by trying things out and repeating if successful.

Tripod grasp – a pencil hold where the finger and thumb hold the pencil, supported by the middle finger.

V

Vet – carry out background checks on a person.

Virus – a cell that takes over others in order to reproduce and so infect the body.

Visual – this describes something that people look at or watch.

Visual prompts – reminding children by showing them an object or an action.

Visual timetable – a series of pictures that help children to understand what is about to happen.

Vitamins – types of nutrients that the body needs in small quantities for good health.

Vocabulary – all the words a person knows.

Vocalisation – making sounds such as babbling and cooing as well as early talk.

W

Weaning – the process by which babies learn to eat food.

Wrap-around care – a service for parents when schools are closed, which includes breakfast club and after-school provision.

Gower College Swansea
Library
Coleg Gŵyr Abertawe
Llyrfgell